PSYCHIATRY – THEORY, APPLICATIONS AND TREATMENTS

AF735640

PERSONALITY DISORDERS

WHAT WE KNOW AND FUTURE DIRECTIONS FOR RESEARCH

PSYCHIATRY – THEORY, APPLICATIONS AND TREATMENTS

Additional books and e-books in this series can be found on Nova's website under the Series tab.

PSYCHIATRY – THEORY, APPLICATIONS AND TREATMENTS

PERSONALITY DISORDERS

WHAT WE KNOW AND FUTURE DIRECTIONS FOR RESEARCH

LEVI I. TRUSLOW
AND
JUSTIN M. RAHMAAN
EDITORS

nova science publishers
New York

Copyright © 2019 by Nova Science Publishers, Inc.

All rights reserved. No part of this book may be reproduced, stored in a retrieval system or transmitted in any form or by any means: electronic, electrostatic, magnetic, tape, mechanical photocopying, recording or otherwise without the written permission of the Publisher.

We have partnered with Copyright Clearance Center to make it easy for you to obtain permissions to reuse content from this publication. Simply navigate to this publication's page on Nova's website and locate the "Get Permission" button below the title description. This button is linked directly to the title's permission page on copyright.com. Alternatively, you can visit copyright.com and search by title, ISBN, or ISSN.

For further questions about using the service on copyright.com, please contact:
Copyright Clearance Center
Phone: +1-(978) 750-8400 Fax: +1-(978) 750-4470 E-mail: info@copyright.com.

NOTICE TO THE READER

The Publisher has taken reasonable care in the preparation of this book, but makes no expressed or implied warranty of any kind and assumes no responsibility for any errors or omissions. No liability is assumed for incidental or consequential damages in connection with or arising out of information contained in this book. The Publisher shall not be liable for any special, consequential, or exemplary damages resulting, in whole or in part, from the readers' use of, or reliance upon, this material. Any parts of this book based on government reports are so indicated and copyright is claimed for those parts to the extent applicable to compilations of such works.

Independent verification should be sought for any data, advice or recommendations contained in this book. In addition, no responsibility is assumed by The Publisher for any injury and/or damage to persons or property arising from any methods, products, instructions, ideas or otherwise contained in this publication.

This publication is designed to provide accurate and authoritative information with regard to the subject matter covered herein. It is sold with the clear understanding that the Publisher is not engaged in rendering legal or any other professional services. If legal or any other expert assistance is required, the services of a competent person should be sought. FROM A DECLARATION OF PARTICIPANTS JOINTLY ADOPTED BY A COMMITTEE OF THE AMERICAN BAR ASSOCIATION AND A COMMITTEE OF PUBLISHERS.

Additional color graphics may be available in the e-book version of this book.

Library of Congress Cataloging-in-Publication Data

ISBN: 978-1-53615-139-8

Published by Nova Science Publishers, Inc. † New York

CONTENTS

PREFACE

Personality Disorders: What We Know and Future Directions For Research first presents an overview of the current *Diagnostic and Statistical Manual of Mental Disorders—5th Edition* conceptualisation of personality disorders. After discussing the strengths and limitations of the *Diagnostic and Statistical Manual of Mental Disorders—5th Edition*'s categorical approach to personality disorder classification, the authors review relevant literature pertaining to the trait and temperament model operationalised in the Schedule for Nonadaptive and Adaptive Personality.

Next, this collection examines dynamic interpersonal processes associated with the etiology and maintenance of personality impairment using an experience sampling methodology and two different data analytic approaches to quantify how patients' perceptions of self and other influence their symptom expression, emotions and functioning in daily life.

The authors study the structural validity of a brief form of the Personality Inventory for DSM-5 in a sample of college students identifying as black/or African American. Consistent with previous research, results suggest that the measure conforms to a higher-order five-factor structure. However, results also indicate that traits are associated with depressive symptoms and alcohol use in different ways than in white samples, suggesting differences in the validity of maladaptive traits across race.

The closing chapter aims to discuss the differences between the clinical constructs of psychopathy and antisocial personality disorder. Specifically, psychopathy and antisocial personality disorder are compared and contrasted via a review of the literature. Subsequent implications for the treatment of criminal behavior are described, and a discussion on future research is provided.

Chapter 1 - This chapter will first present an overview of the current DSM-5 conceptualisation of personality disorders (PDs). After discussing the strengths and limitations of the DSM-5's categorical approach to PD classification, this chapter will then review relevant literature pertaining to the use of a specific dimensional trait model in the conceptualisation of PDs, namely the trait and temperament model operationalised in the Schedule for Nonadaptive and Adaptive Personality (SNAP). Lastly, directions for future researched are discussed.

Chapter 2 - Although contemporary conceptualizations of personality pathology define it as a disorder of perceiving self and others and relating self to others, research on the effects of interpersonal perception in personality disorders is limited. Utilizing the interpersonal situation framework, this chapter presents two analytic methods for investigating the associations between patients' interpersonal perception and their symptom expression, emotions, and functioning in daily life. Psychotherapy outpatients (N = 57) used smartphones to complete event-contingent surveys assessing perceptions of self and other, emotional states, symptoms, and functioning after every face-to-face social interaction lasting more than 3 minutes over the course of 21 days. The first approach to the data employs multilevel modeling analyses to examine severity of personality impairment as a moderator of associations between interpersonal perception and psychological state. These findings help to move the field of personality pathology beyond cross-sectional description and classification by providing information on dynamic patient functioning in daily life. However, these inferences can only be applied to populations as a whole and may not apply to specific individuals. The second approach to the data extends these findings by applying person specific analyses to describe the interpersonal dynamics for three individual patients from the sample. Examining how interpersonal perception relates to psychological states for specific individuals demonstrates the efficacy and utility of a person specific analytic approach and illustrates how findings at the person level can and do differ from findings at the population level. We discuss the implications for understanding personality pathology from an interpersonal perspective and suggest future directions using these methods.

Chapter 3 - There has been increased interest in conceptualizing and assessing personality disorders in terms of maladaptive personality traits. Recent research in this domain has focused on a specific instrument for measuring maladaptive trails, the *Personality Inventory for DSM-5* (PID-5), which was developed for the formal trait model listed in Section III of DSM-5. Although a growing number of studies have suggested the structural and criterion validity of the traits measured by the PID-5, these studies used almost exclusively White samples. Research has been perhaps most notably absent on individuals identifying as Black/African American, who constitute the largest racial minority group in the U.S. In this study we examine the structural and criterion validity of a brief form of the PID-5 in a sample of college students identifying as Black/African American. Consistent with previous research, results suggest that the measure conforms to a higher-order five-factor structure. However, results also indicate that traits are associated with depressive symptoms and alcohol use in different ways than in White samples, suggesting differences in the criterion validity of maladaptive traits across race. These findings have ramifications for the assessment of maladaptive traits cross-culturally and point toward directions for future research.

Chapter 4 - This chapter aims to discuss the differences between the clinical constructs of psychopathy and antisocial personality disorder. Specifically, this chapter will first compare and contrast psychopathy and antisocial personality disorder via a review of the literature and will argue that these terms reflect different constructs. Next, this chapter will discuss the subsequent implications for the treatment for criminal behaviour. The chapter concludes with a discussion on avenues of future research.

In: Personality Disorders
Editors: Levi I. Truslow et al.
ISBN: 978-1-53615-139-8
© 2019 Nova Science Publishers, Inc.

Chapter 1

UNDERSTANDING PERSONALITY DISORDERS USING DIMENSIONAL PERSONALITY TRAIT MODELS

Ninawa Butrus*
Private Practice, Melbourne, Australia

ABSTRACT

This chapter will first present an overview of the current DSM-5 conceptualisation of personality disorders (PDs). After discussing the strengths and limitations of the DSM-5's categorical approach to PD classification, this chapter will then review relevant literature pertaining to the use of a specific dimensional trait model in the conceptualisation of PDs, namely the trait and temperament model operationalised in the Schedule for Nonadaptive and Adaptive Personality (SNAP). Lastly, directions for future researched are discussed.

Keywords: personality disorder, personality, personality traits, dimensional models, maladaptive traits

---

* Corresponding Author Email: nbutrus@hotmail.com.

INTRODUCTION

During the last two decades, critics of the *Diagnostic and Statistical Manual of Mental Disorders*, which is now in its fifth edition, (DSM-5; American Psychiatric Association [APA], 2013) and the tenth edition of the *International Statistical Classification of Diseases and Related Health Problems* (ICD-10; World Health Organization [WHO], 1992) Personality Disorder (PD) nosology have become increasingly vocal in their calls for a dimensional alternative to the problematic categorical classification system. This chapter will present an overview of the current DSM-5 conceptualisation of Personality Disorders (PDs). After discussing the strengths and limitations of the DSM-5's categorical approach to PD classification, this chapter will then review relevant literature pertaining to the use of a particular dimensional trait model in the conceptualisation of PDs namely, the trait and temperament model operationalised in the Schedule for Nonadaptive and Adaptive Personality (SNAP).

PERSONALITY DISORDERS

The Personality Disorders (PDs) are an intriguing, yet controversial group of mental disorders that are contained within the official psychiatric nosology. Although personality pathology has been recognised throughout history (Millon, 2011) and in each edition of the DSM (Oldham, 2009), the publication of DSM-III (APA, 1980) saw the birth of contemporary nosological formulations of PDs. DSM-III provided explicit diagnostic criteria sets for each PD and introduced a multiaxial format that saw PDs placed on a separate axis (Axis II) from the episodic psychiatric disorders (Axis I) (Widiger, 2001). Further refinements and changes to the PD diagnostic criteria were made in DSM-III-R (APA, 1987), DSM-IV (APA, 1994) and DSM-IV-TR (APA, 2000) with changes in the latter carrying over into the current version, that is, the DSM-5 (APA, 2013). In this chapter, references to DSM-IV-TR and DSM-5 may be used interchangeably since the PD criteria and conceptualisation across these latter versions of the DSM are identical.

DSM-5 Conceptualisation of PDs

The DSM-5 continues the DSM-III's nosological tradition of classifying PDs as distinct diagnostic categories. With its roots in Kraeplinian assumptions about mental illness, the DSM-5 is based on a medical model in that it delineates boundaries between normality and abnormality and conceptualises all mental disorders as discrete medical conditions (Trull & Durrett, 2005). According to the DSM-5, PDs are "qualitatively distinct clinical syndromes" (APA, 2013, p. 646) that resemble disease states and are conceptualised as being either present or absent in an individual. In this scheme, the presence or absence of symptoms of pathology, as determined by specific sets of behavioural criteria, is the primary consideration for diagnosticians because it is assumed that any observed criterion symptoms reflect manifestations of an individual's underlying maladaptive personality (Saulsman & Page, 2004).

The DSM-5 defines a PD as an enduring, pervasive and inflexible pattern of inner experience and behaviour that deviates from cultural norms and leads to distress or impairments in functioning (APA, 2013). The DSM-5 definition elaborates that this enduring pattern of inner experience and behaviour must be manifested in at least two out of four areas of functioning: cognition, affectivity, interpersonal behaviour and impulse control. Distorted cognition and interpersonal problems are arguably typical features of all PDs, whereas affective and impulse control problems can be viewed along a continuum depending on the PD category in question (Skodol, 2009).

The DSM-5 defines PDs in terms of personality traits but specifies that it is only when personality traits are "inflexible and maladaptive" and cause either "significant functional impairment" or "subjective distress" that they then constitute a PD (APA, 2013, p. 647). As Livesley (2001) pointed out, this definition implies a trait-based dimensional continuity between normal and maladaptive personality functioning. However, there is a striking disjunction between the DSM-5's trait-based definition of PDs and the diagnostic criteria used to assess PDs (Krueger et al., 2011). That is, the DSM-5 PD criteria are not "personality traits" per se. Rather, the PD criteria are a mixture of specific behavioural acts, psychological symptoms and other manifestations of underlying personality traits that are presumed to comprise the relevant categorical PD syndrome (Skodol, Clark, et al., 2011).

The DSM-5 recognises 10 PD categories and groups them into three separate clusters based on their descriptive similarities (APA, 2013). Cluster A, the odd/eccentric cluster, includes the paranoid, schizoid and schizotypal PDs. Cluster B, the dramatic/emotional/erratic cluster, includes the histrionic, narcissistic, antisocial and borderline PDs. Finally, Cluster C, the anxious/fearful cluster, includes the avoidant, dependent and obsessive-compulsive PDs. The DSM-5 also contains an Other Specified Personality Disorder and Unspecified Personality Disorder category. The DSM-5's classification of PDs is generally comparable with that of the ICD-10 (WHO, 1992), however there are some notable differences. For example, the ICD-10 nosology does not recognise narcissistic PD and it includes schizotypal PD in the section for schizophrenia and other psychotic disorders rather than in the PD section.

In order to qualify for a DSM-5 PD diagnosis, an individual must meet the general diagnostic criteria for a PD and the criteria for at least one of the 10 PD categories or the other/unspecified category. Each DSM-5 PD is assessed by between seven and nine diagnostic criteria and multiple PD diagnoses are permitted. As with other mental disorders in the DSM-5, the diagnostic criteria for the PDs are polythetic. That is, only a subset of the criteria for each PD needs to be met in order to reach the threshold for a diagnosis. For example, a diagnosis of avoidant PD requires that any four out of a possible seven diagnostic criteria are met (APA, 2013).

Strengths and Limitations of the DSM-5's Categorical Model of PDs

As outlined by Widiger and Frances (2002), the DSM-5's categorical system of classifying PDs has three commonly cited strengths. First, diagnostic categories have a long history in the official psychiatric classification systems and, therefore, are familiar to clinicians and researchers. Indeed, the categorical classification of mental disorders is fundamental to the neo-Kraeplinian approach to psychiatric nosology (Livesley, 2001) and a departure from categorical diagnostic rubrics would be a paradigm shift for the fields of psychiatry and clinical psychology (Widiger & Frances, 2002).

Second, diagnostic categories are easy to use. It is easier for clinicians and researchers to determine that an individual either has or does not have a PD and to communicate this categorical diagnosis to others than it is to diagnose a PD based on: (a) a profile of the degrees to which various PDs are present; or (b) multiple trait dimensions (Widiger & Frances, 2002). As noted by Frances (1993), the labels associated with categorical PD diagnoses, such as paranoid, are relatively straightforward and can rapidly convey a vivid description of an individual that may otherwise be lost in a multifaceted dimensional profile.

Finally, categorical diagnoses are consistent with clinical decision-making. Widiger and Frances (2002) observed that many clinical decisions are made in a categorical way and hence are facilitated by a categorical model of classification. For instance, clinicians must decide whether a PD is present or not, whether medication is indicated or not, whether hospitalisation is required or not, and so on.

In spite of its strengths, there are numerous well-documented problems with the DSM-5's categorical system of classifying PDs (Clark, Watson, & Reynolds, 1995; Jablensky, 2002; Trull & Durrett, 2005; Widiger, 2007; Widiger & Samuel, 2005; Widiger & Trull, 2007). Five key limitations have been repeatedly highlighted in the literature and are particularly noteworthy. The first limitation is excessive diagnostic co-occurrence amongst the PD categories. Research has shown that individuals who met the diagnostic criteria for one PD are also highly likely to meet the diagnostic criteria for other PDs (Coid, Yang, Tyrer, Roberts, & Ullrich, 2006; Fossati et al., 2000; Zimmerman, Rothschild, & Chelminski, 2005). Excessive diagnostic co-occurrence suggests a problematic level of overlap in the PD diagnostic criteria sets and calls into question the specificity and discriminant validity of the PD categories (Bornstein, 1998; Samuel & Widiger, 2010; Widiger & Samuel, 2005).

The second limitation is inadequate coverage of personality pathology. Studies have consistently shown that Personality Disorder Not Otherwise Specified (PDNOS) is one of the most prevalent PD diagnoses (Chanen et al., 2004; Verheul, Bartak, & Widiger, 2007; Verheul & Widiger, 2004) and that individuals with PDNOS diagnoses experience similar dysfunctional outcomes to those with any of the recognised Cluster A, B or C PDs (Johnson, First, Cohen, & Skodol, 2005). The high prevalence of dysfunctional PDNOS diagnoses accordingly suggests that the DSM-5's existing PD classification fails to adequately capture or describe the possible range of personality pathology (Widiger & Trull, 2007). As Widiger (2007) noted, increased coverage of personality pathology in the DSM-5 could be achieved by adding more PD categories; however, this would then have the drawback of exacerbating the aforementioned problem with excessive diagnostic co-occurrence.

The third limitation is the arbitrary and unstable boundary between normal and abnormal personality functioning. The DSM-5 provides no justification for the different thresholds that are required to be met in order to derive each PD diagnosis (Widiger & Trull, 2007). Furthermore, the diagnostic criteria for each PD are not equally weighted in terms of their severity or maladaptivity, thus simply counting the number of criteria that an individual meets appears to be an imperfect method for deriving a PD diagnosis (Bornstein, 2011). To illustrate this drawback, it is unclear how an individual who meets five out of the nine criteria for a diagnosis of narcissistic PD would differ in important clinical respects from an individual who meets four (subthreshold) or six (diagnosis present) of the diagnostic criteria. What is clear is that the DSM-5's categorical model wherein PDs must be diagnosed as either present or absent leads to a loss of information regarding subthreshold cases (Zimmerman, 2012). Interestingly, the few taxometric analyses of PDs that have been conducted with adult samples have generally failed to find clear evidence of distinct PD taxons, with the exception of a possible schizotypy taxon that encompasses a broad range of schizophrenia-spectrum psychopathology (Haslam, Holland, & Kuppens, 2012; Haslam & Williams, 2006). Such findings further call into question the validity of the DSM-5's categorical model of PDs.

The fourth limitation is excessive heterogeneity within PD categories. As discussed previously, the criteria sets for the DSM-5 PD categories are polythetic in that only a subset of the diagnostic criteria is required to be met in order to receive a PD diagnosis. However, polythetic criteria sets produce a great deal of heterogeneity within PD categories that critics have questioned whether the existing PD categories do actually represent qualitatively distinct disorders as purported by the DSM-5 (Trull & Durrett, 2005; Widiger & Trull, 2007). For instance, there are 256 ways that an individual can meet the diagnostic criteria for borderline PD as the DSM-5 requires that any combination of five out of nine criteria be met to reach the threshold for a diagnosis. Clearly, not all individuals who meet the criteria for this diagnosis would be alike with respect to their symptomology and this consequently could have implications for the treatment that is provided. Perhaps more remarkable is the fact that any two individuals with a diagnosis of obsessive-compulsive PD need not share any diagnostic criteria since only four out of eight criteria are required to be met in order to receive the diagnosis (APA, 2013).

The fifth limitation is poor reliability of PD diagnoses. Research has shown that the DSM-5 PDs are not reliably diagnosed in clinical practice (Widiger, 2007). Furthermore, existing PD measures, especially self-report measures, are limited by serious deficits in test-retest, inter-rater and inter-measure reliability (Clark & Harrison, 2001). This is in contrast to measures of personality dimensions, such as traits, which typically are more reliable (Clark & Harrison, 2001).

Dimensional Models of PDs

An alternative to the DSM-5's categorical approach to conceptualising PDs is a dimensional model of classification. Whereas categorical models classify personality pathology in terms of discrete diagnostic categories, dimensional models conceptualise personality pathology as varying along multiple continuous dimensions (Livesley, 2001). A dimensional approach to PD classification has many advantages over the existing categorical approach. Some commonly cited advantages of dimensional models include increased coverage of the range of personality pathology, resolution of the categorical classification problems of excessive diagnostic co-occurrence and within-category heterogeneity, and improved diagnostic reliability (Trull & Durrett, 2005; Widiger, 2007; Widiger & Frances, 2002; Widiger & Trull, 2007). Other advantages include the increased retention of information regarding subthreshold cases and greater diagnostic flexibility (Widiger & Frances, 2002). Whilst many clinicians and researchers support the use of a dimensional model for PD classification, there is a lack of agreement as to its precise format (Bernstein, Iscan, & Maser, 2007; Frances, 1993; Spitzer, First, Shedler, West, & Skodol, 2008). For instance, Widiger and Simonsen (2005) conducted a review of the literature and found no less than 18 proposals of alternative dimensional models of PD classification for DSM-5.

In 2011 the DSM-5 PD Work Group published a revised version of their initial proposed reformulation of the PD classification (Skodol, Bender, et al., 2011; Skodol, Clark, et al., 2011). The Work Group's current proposal is a hybrid categorical-dimensional model of PD classification that focuses on impairments in personality functioning and the presence of pathological personality traits in a revised definition of PD (APA, 2012c). This proposed PD model has three main components (APA, 2012d). The first component is a 5-point Levels of Personality Functioning Scale which diagnosticians must use to rate the severity of personality dysfunction based on the degree of impairment in self (identity and self-direction) and interpersonal (empathy and intimacy) domains (APA, 2012b). The second component is recognition of six specific PD types (antisocial, avoidant, borderline, narcissistic, obsessive-compulsive and schizotypal) and a PD Trait Specified (PDTS) type that replaces the DSM-5's PDNOS category and excluded PDs (paranoid, schizoid, histrionic and dependent). Each proposed DSM-5 PD type has its own set of diagnostic criteria, all of which consist of core impairments in personality functioning and unique combinations of pathological personality traits that define the disorder (APA, 2012a). The third component is a hierarchical dimensional trait model that consists of five higher-order trait domains (Negative Affectivity, Detachment, Antagonism, Disinhibition and Psychoticism), each of which subsume between three and nine lower-order pathological facet traits of which there are 25 in total (APA, 2012d; Krueger, Derringer, Markon, Watson, & Skodol, 2012). It is proposed that diagnosticians rate the five domains and 25 facet traits on a 4-point scale of descriptiveness (APA, 2012d). As mentioned above, each PD type is comprised of a designated combination of pathological traits which must be rated as part of the diagnostic criteria for that PD. However, if an individual does not meet the criteria for one of the six PD types but does meet the revised general criteria for a PD (APA, 2012a), then a diagnosis of PDTS is given whereby a profile of the individual's elevated pathological traits is recorded (APA, 2012c). In order to facilitate the transition from the DSM-5's categorical PD model to the DSM-5's hybrid categorical-dimensional model of PD classification, the Work Group has assigned the combinations of pathological traits that are said to define each DSM-5 PD category (APA, 2011).

Arguably, the most significant aspect of the DSM-5's proposed revision to the PD classification is the use of a dimensional trait model that links constellations of traits to specific PD types (APA, 2011). The dimensional trait component of the DSM-5's proposed model grounds both the definition and diagnosis of PD in a trait-based system, which is in line with dimensional trait models of PDs (Skodol, Clark, et al., 2011). As Tackett et al. (2009) pointed out, rather than using a cumbersome set of overlapping diagnostic criteria for each PD category, a smaller set of universal personality trait dimensions could be used to identify and define PD prototypes that have clinical, research or theoretical importance. In a dimensional trait system of PDs, many multidimensional profile configurations are possible because each individual will obtain his or her own profile of prominent traits (Skodol, 2011). Therefore, trait dimensions could be useful for differentiating variants of broad-based personality pathology constructs, such as the grandiose and vulnerable expressions of narcissism (Miller et al., 2010; Pincus & Lukowitsky, 2010) or the primary and secondary characteristics of psychopathy (Ross, Lutz, & Bailley, 2004). The DSM-5 PD Work Group emphasised that their proposed model is undergoing empirical validation and could be further revised (APA, 2012d; Skodol, Clark, et al., 2011). Indeed, the proposed model was published in the appendix of DSM-5 as requiring further study (APA, 2013).

DIMENSIONAL TRAIT MODELS OF PDS

Dimensional trait models do not conceptualise PDs as discrete categories. Instead, PDs are conceptualised as representing extreme and dysfunctional variants of continuous personality traits (Widiger & Frances, 2002). Dimensional trait models of PDs identify the particular combinations of personality traits that underlie the features, symptoms or behavioural manifestations of personality pathology and reconceptualise PDs using these trait dimensions (Widiger, Costa, & McCrae, 2002; Widiger, Livesley, & Clark, 2009; Widiger & Mullins-Sweatt, 2009). To date, the comprehensive and widely-validated Five-Factor Model (FFM) of personality has generated the most empirical research as a dimensional alternative to DSM-5's PD classification (see Butrus & Witenberg, 2015; Samuel & Widiger, 2008; Saulsman & Page, 2004; Widiger & Mullins-Sweatt, 2009). Another promising dimensional trait model of PDs that has received increased research attention is the trait and temperament model operationalised in the Schedule for Nonadaptive and Adaptive Personality (SNAP), which will be discussed next.

The SNAP Model of Maladaptive Personality Traits

The trait and temperament model operationalised in the SNAP is an empirically-derived model of maladaptive personality traits that was developed by linking Big Three models of general personality traits (see Clark & Watson, 2008) with psychopathology through the set of dimensions that emerged from an analysis of DSM-III/III-R criteria (L.A. Clark, personal communication, November 13, 2008).

Developed by Clark (1993), the SNAP is the end-product of a series of studies that aimed to identify the specific trait and temperament dimensions relevant to personality dysfunction. As outlined in Clark, Simms, Wu, and Casillas (in press), raters sorted the diagnostic criteria for DSM-III/III-R PDs and other PD-like constructs (e.g., dysthymia) into synonym categories and scores from the resultant co-occurrence matrix were subjected to factor-analysis. A 22-factor solution of criterion clusters was retained whereby: (a) each cluster contained criterion symptoms from at least two diagnostic categories; and (b) the full criteria for each diagnostic category did not aggregate into a single cluster (Clark et al., in press). These findings indicated that the personality pathology dimensions that comprised the criterion clusters were common to the various PD and PD-like categories, thus confirming the problem of diagnostic criteria overlap in categorical models of PD (Clark, McEwen, Collard, & Hickok, 1993; Clark, Vorhies, & McEwan, 2002). Items were subsequently developed to assess the criterion clusters and were administered to clinical and non-clinical samples. Item scores were factor-analysed and 12 primary traits emerged (Clark, 1993). Clark also incorporated the Big Three temperament dimensions of Negative Temperament, Positive Temperament and Disinhibition from the General Temperament Survey (Clark & Watson, 1990) into the SNAP so as to measure aspects of normal-range personality (Clark et al., in press). Subsequent factor-analytic research suggested a hierarchical structure for the SNAP, whereby all of the primary trait scales loaded with one of the temperament scales (Clark et al., in press; Clark et al., 2002; Simms & Clark, 2006). However, it is important to note that the SNAP higher-order temperament scales are independent dimensions and are not composites of the lower-order primary trait scales. The SNAP instrument is now in its second edition and the SNAP-2 (Clark et al., in press). Clark et al. (in press) reported that the items that comprise the SNAP and SNAP-2 trait and temperament scales remain the same across both versions of the instrument. For clarity, the term "SNAP" will be used in this chapter to refer to the trait and temperament scales common to both versions of the instrument and when discussing previous research; whereas the term "SNAP-2" will be used when discussing aspects pertaining only to the new SNAP-2 instrument. Table 1 contains a description of the SNAP maladaptive personality traits.

The SNAP has links with other personality trait models. Research has shown that the SNAP's Big Three higher-order temperament dimensions of Negative Temperament, Positive Temperament and Disinhibition correlate with corresponding higher-order dimensions from the FFM, that is, the Neuroticism, Extraversion and low Conscientiousness/ Agreeableness domains, respectively, indicating convergent validity (Clark et al., in press; Clark et al., 2002; Simms & Clark, 2006). Research has also shown that the temperament dimensions assessed by the SNAP and other Big Three models relate to psychological disorders in similar ways to their counterpart FFM domains (Clark, 2005; Kotov, Gamez, Schmidt, & Watson, 2010; Watson, Clark, & Carey, 1988; Watson, Kotov, & Gamez, 2006). Furthermore, Clark and Livesley (2002) discovered strong convergence between the SNAP and a similar measure of maladaptive personality traits known as the Dimensional Assessment of Personality Pathology (DAPP; Livesley, 2006). In fact, when the SNAP and DAPP were factor-analysed together a variation of the FFM structure emerged, but without the Openness domain (Clark, Livesley, Schroeder, & Irish, 1996). Some work has suggested that trait dimensions from various Big Trait models, such as the FFM, SNAP and DAPP, can be integrated within a common hierarchical trait structure to maximally assess normal and abnormal personality characteristics (Markon, Krueger, & Watson, 2005; Samuel, Simms, Clark, Livesley, & Widiger, 2010; Widiger et al., 2009; Widiger & Simonsen, 2005).

Table 1. Description of the SNAP Maladaptive Personality Traits

SNAP Trait	Description
Negative Temperament	*The tendency to experience a wide range of negative emotions and to overreact to minor stress.*
Mistrust	Pervasive suspiciousness and cynical attitude towards others.
Manipulativeness	Egocentric willingness to exploit/manipulate for personal gain without regard for others' rights or feelings.
Aggression	Reflects individual differences in the frequency and intensity of the experience of anger and its behavioural expression of aggression.
Self-Harm	Tendency to self-harm in the context of self-loathing.
Low Self-Esteem	Reflects negative beliefs about one's self-worth.
Suicide Proneness	Tendency to experience self-destructive thoughts and behaviours.
Eccentric Perceptions	Tendency to experience unusual somatosensory perceptions, cognitions and beliefs.
Dependency	Reflects individual differences in self-reliance, locus of control and self-confidence in decision-making.
Positive Temperament	*The tendency to experience a wide range of positive emotions and to be pleasurably, actively and effectively involved in one's life.*
Exhibitionism	Tendency to engage in overt attention-seeking versus withdrawal from attention.
Entitlement	Tendency to have unrealistically positive self-regard and the feeling that one should receive special treatment versus a humble, self-effacing attitude.
Detachment	Tendency towards emotional and interpersonal distance.
Disinhibition	*The tendency to behave in an under-controlled versus an over-controlled manner.*
Impulsivity	Tendency to act on a momentary basis without an overall plan versus the tendency to stop and think before acting.
Propriety	Reflects a preference for traditional, conservative morality versus the rejection of social rules and convention.
Workaholism	Reflects individual differences in attitudes towards work and leisure, a tendency to perfectionism, and self-imposed demands for excellence.

Note. Adapted from Clark et al. (in press).

The SNAP and PDs

Whereas using the FFM to conceptualise PDs is a top-down approach because it applies an existing model of personality traits to understanding PDs, the SNAP approach to conceptualising PDs is a bottom-up strategy (Clark & Livesley, 2002). That is, the SNAP was developed by first examining the inter-relationships amongst the criterion symptoms of existing PDs and PD-like constructs and then formulating a dimensional trait model that represented each criterion cluster of personality pathology that emerged (Clark & Livesley, 2002). Clark (1993) hypothesised specific conceptual relationships between PD categories and SNAP maladaptive personality traits. These hypothesised directional relationships are listed in Table 2.

Table 2. Hypothesised Directional Relationships between DSM-5 PDs and SNAP Maladaptive Traits

SNAP Traits	**PAR**	**SZD**	**SZT**	**ATS**	**BDL**	**HST**	**NAR**	**AVD**	**DEP**	**OBC**
Negative Temperament					+			+	+	+
Mistrust	+	+	+					+		
Manipulativeness				+			+			
Aggression	+			+	+					
Self-Harm					+				+	
Eccentric Perceptions			+							
Dependency									+	
Positive Temperament						+		−		
Exhibitionism						+	+			
Entitlement				+		+	+			
Detachment		+	+					+		
Disinhibition				+						
Impulsivity				+	+	+				
Propriety										+
Workaholism										+

Note. PAR = paranoid PD; SZD = schizoid PD; SZT = schizotypal PD; ATS = antisocial PD; BDL = borderline PD; HST = histrionic PD; NAR = narcissistic PD; AVD = avoidant PD; DEP = dependent PD; OBC = obsessive-compulsive PD. + indicates a hypothesised positive relationship; while −indicates a hypothesised negative relationship. Hypothesised directional relationships are based on the PD-SNAP trait conceptual profiles put forth by Clark (1993).

Given that the SNAP is embedded in and is a measure of personality pathology, it is surprising that there are so few published studies that have examined the relationships between PDs and SNAP maladaptive personality traits. Table 3 contains a brief overview of some of the key published studies that have examined relationships between all 10 PDs and

SNAP traits. As summarised in the table, moderate to strong support was obtained in all studies for the conceptually matched PD-SNAP trait relationships hypothesised by Clark (1993). However, the PD-SNAP trait correlations in the studies that reported them were predominantly below $r = .45$, thus generally in the small to medium effect size range (Cohen, 1988). Moreover, the three studies that used regression analyses (Morey et al., 2003; Reynolds & Clark, 2001; Wolf, Harrington, & Miller, 2011) revealed that SNAP traits explained generally a moderate amount of variance in PDs, irrespective of whether all or only a subset of SNAP traits were entered as predictor variables. Overall, these results support the idea that PDs can be conceptualised using dimensions of personality pathology as operationalised in the SNAP model.

Key Limitations in Conceptualising PDs Using the SNAP Dimensional Trait Model

The literature that has been reviewed thus far has demonstrated that PDs can be understood as constellations of extreme and maladaptive variants of traits from the SNAP. However, conceptualising PDs using this dimensional trait model is not without its limitations.

A key limitation in using the SNAP to conceptualise PDs is that, given its method of development, the SNAP trait dimensions may correspond too closely to existing DSM PD categories and, therefore, fail to identify variants of personality pathology that are not covered by the DSM classification (Trull & Durrett, 2005). For instance, critics could argue that the SNAP maladaptive traits of Dependency and Exhibitionism are simply "dimensionalised" variants of the DSM dependent and histrionic PD categories, respectively. However, at least one study has found SNAP traits to be useful for conceptualising non-DSM variants of personality pathology, that is, psychopathy (Pryor, Miller, & Gaughan, 2009).

Another limitation in conceptualising PDs using the SNAP is that traits from this dimensional trait model account for only a modest proportion of variance in measures of PDs, even when examined with FFM traits, thus limiting the ability of either model to explain personality pathology as currently defined by the DSM-5 (Clark, 2007; Wright, 2011).

Table 3. Overview of Some Key Published Studies on the Relationships between PDs and SNAP Traits

Study	Sample	PD Measure	Key Findings
Clark (1993)	89 outpatients & inpatients	SIDP-R (DSM-III-R PDs)	• *Correlations:* Strong support for most PD-SNAP trait relationships hypothesised by Clark (1993); weak support for predictions involving obsessive-compulsive PD.
Reynolds & Clark (2001)[a]	94 outpatients & inpatients	SIDP-IV	• *Regressions:* All 15 SNAP traits explained between 28% (schizotypal PD) and 57% (borderline and avoidant PDs) of the variance across PDs. • *Regressions:* SNAP traits hypothesised by Clark (1993) to be related to each PD explained between 21% (schizotypal and histrionic PDs) and 52% (borderline PD) of the variance across PDs.
Hurt & Oltmanns (2002)	157 incarcerated women	SNAP (DSM-III-R PDs)	• *Correlations:* Most PD-SNAP trait relationships proposed by Clark (1993) were confirmed; weak support for predictions involving histrionic PD.
Morey et al. (2003)	529 outpatients	DIPD-IV	• *Correlations:* Most PD-SNAP trait relationships proposed by Clark (1993) were confirmed. • *Regressions:* All 15 SNAP traits significantly explained the following amounts of variance in four PDs: 43.6% for borderline PD, 27.8% for schizotypal PD, 38.97% for avoidant PD and 26.7% for obsessive-compulsive PD.
Miller, Reynolds, & Pilkonis (2004)[a]	94 outpatients & inpatients	SIDP-IV	• *Correlations:* Strong support for the PD-SNAP trait relationships predicted by Clark (1993).
Miller et al. (2010)	130 outpatients	Ratings of DSM-5 PD criteria	• *Correlations:* Modest support for the PD-SNAP trait relationships predicted by Clark (1993); weak support for predictions involving schizoid, schizotypal, histrionic, avoidant and obsessive-compulsive PDs.
Clark et al. (in press)[a]	94 outpatients & inpatients	SIDP-IV	• *Correlations:* Strong support for the PD-SNAP trait relationships hypothesised by Clark (1993).

Study	Sample	PD Measure	*Key Findings*
Wolf, Harrington, & Miller (2011)	86 military veterans with PTSD	IPDE	• *Correlations:* Modest support for the predicted PD-SNAP trait relationships proposed by Clark (1993); all PDs except dependent PD had at least one predicted relationship that was not confirmed. • *Regressions:* All 15 SNAP traits explained between 24% (obsessive-compulsive PD) to 46% (schizoid PD) of the variance in PDs.

Note. PTSD = Post-Traumatic Stress Disorder. SIDP-R = Structured Interview for DSM-III-R Personality (Pfohl, Blum, Zimmerman, & Stangl, 1989); SIDP-IV = Structured Interview for DSM-IV Personality (Pfohl, Blum, & Zimmerman, 1997); SNAP = Schedule for Nonadaptive and Adaptive Personality (Clark, 1993); DIPD-IV = Diagnostic Interview for DSM-IV Personality Disorders (Zanarini, Frankenberg, Sickel, & Yong, 1996); IPDE = International Personality Disorder Examination (Loranger, 1999).

[a] Appears to be the same dataset.

To date, two key published studies have examined the incremental validity of both higher- and lower-order SNAP and FFM traits in predicting variance in DSM-5 PD features. These studies will be described next.

The first study, by Reynolds and Clark (2001), involved a mixed clinical sample of 94 outpatients and inpatients. Hierarchical regression analyses revealed that the FFM domains on an average explained 27% of variance in PDs, while all 15 SNAP traits incrementally explained an average of 22% of additional variance. In the reverse entry, all 15 SNAP traits on an average explained 45% of variance across PDs, while the FFM domains incrementally explained an average of 4% of additional variance. Altogether, the FFM domains and SNAP traits on an average explained 49% of total variance in PDs, which ranged from 30% (schizotypal PD) to 63% (avoidant PD). Reynolds and Clark also examined the incremental validity of specific lower-order traits from the hypothesised PD-FFM facet trait profiles proposed by Widiger, Trull, Clarkin, Sanderson, and Costa (1994) and the hypothesised PD-SNAP trait relationships put forth by Clark (1993), respectively, to predict variance in their corresponding PDs. The selected FFM facets from the Widiger et al. profiles explained an average of 35% of variance in PDs, while the selected SNAP traits from the Clark profiles incrementally added an average 8% of additional variance. In the reverse entry, the selected SNAP traits from the Clark profiles on an average explained 32% of variance in PDs, whereas the selected FFM facets from the Widiger et al. profiles on an average explained an additional 10% of incremental variance. Altogether, the selected FFM and SNAP lower-order traits from both the Widiger et al. and Clark profiles on an average explained 42% of the total variance in PDs, which ranged from 25% (schizotypal PD) to 64% (avoidant PD).

The second study, by Stepp, Trull, Burr, Wolfenstein, and Vieth (2005), examined only borderline, antisocial and histrionic PDs and involved a combined sample of 200 clinical and non-clinical participants. Hierarchical regression analyses revealed that the FFM domains on an average explained about 22% of the variance across the three PDs, while the three SNAP temperaments incrementally explained on average less than one per cent of additional variance. In the reverse entry, the SNAP temperaments on an average explained 20% of the variance in PDs, while the FFM domains on an average explained 9% of incremental variance. Altogether, the FFM domains and SNAP temperaments on an average explained approximately 29% of total variance in measures of the three PDs, ranging from 22% (histrionic PD) to 33% (borderline PD). Stepp and colleagues also examined the incremental validity of lower-order traits from the hypothesised PD-FFM facet trait profiles proposed by Trull and Widiger (1997) and the PD-SNAP trait profiles put forth by Clark (1993), respectively, to predict variance in the three PDs. Selected FFM facets from the Trull and Widiger PD-FFM facet trait profiles on an average explained 31% of the variance in PDs, while selected SNAP traits from Clark's PD-SNAP trait profiles explained an average 4% of additional variance. In the reverse entry, SNAP traits from the Clark profiles on an average explained 23% of the variance in PDs, whereas FFM facets from the Trull and Widiger profiles on an average explained 13% of incremental variance. Together, the selected FFM and SNAP lower-order traits from both Trull and Widiger's and Clark's hypothesised profiles on an average explained 36% of total variance in these three PDs, ranging from 26% (histrionic PD) to 46% (borderline PD).

It has been argued that a dimensional trait model of PDs should in the first instance be empirically and conceptually linked to the current DSM-5 PD classification in order to replace it (Gunderson, 2010; Samuel & Widiger, 2011; Schmidt, Wagner, & Kiesler, 1993). It is clear from the research reviewed thus far that the sizeable amounts of unexplained variance in measures of the PD categories indicate that SNAP traits do not provide a comprehensive account of the personality pathology features and symptomology that is currently encoded in the DSM-5 PD categories. As such, reconceptualising PDs solely using traits from this dimensional trait model may provide inadequate coverage of maladaptive personality functioning. Thus, the question remains as to what else besides personality traits can account for the variance in PD features?

Future Directions

Further research that explores the SNAP and alternative dimensional models for conceptualising PDs is required. Some potential areas for further research include:

- validating the proposed DSM-5 dimensional PD model
- using SNAP and FFM trait models to conceptualise PDs across diverse samples (e.g., clinical, outpatient, inpatient, forensic)
- exploring what else besides traits can account for variance in PDs (e.g., dysfunctional schemas, defence mechanisms, mentalizing capacity)
- exploring the links between adaptive and maladaptive personality traits and specific functional impairments
- exploring how dimensional trait models can be used to develop treatment programs for PDs
- exploring whether treatment can reduce/change maladaptive personality traits over time.

Conclusion

This chapter presented an overview of the current DSM-5 conceptualisation of PDs and discussed the strengths and limitations of the DSM-5's categorical approach to PD classification. This chapter then described a specific dimensional trait model in the conceptualisation of PDs, namely the trait and temperament model operationalised in the SNAP, and reviewed the key literature pertaining to this model in conceptualising PDs. Suggestions for further research on using dimensional trait models to conceptualise PDs were also provided.

References

American Psychiatric Association. (1980). *Diagnostic and Statistical Manual of Mental Disorders* (3rd ed.). Washington, DC: Author.

American Psychiatric Association. (1987). *Diagnostic and Statistical Manual of Mental Disorders* (3rd revised ed.). Washington, DC: Author.

American Psychiatric Association. (1994). *Diagnostic and Statistical Manual of Mental Disorders* (4th ed.). Washington, DC: Author.

American Psychiatric Association. (2011). *DSM-5 Type and trait cross-walk.* Retrieved November 14, 2011, from http://www.dsm5.org/ProposedRevisions/Pages/DSM-5TypeandTraitCross-Walk.aspx.

American Psychiatric Association. (2012a). *DSM-IV and DSM-5 criteria comparison.* Retrieved June 1, 2012, from http://www.dsm5.org/Documents/PersonalityDisorders/DSM-IVandDSM-5CriteriaforthePersonalityDisorders5-1-12.pdf.

American Psychiatric Association. (2012b). *Levels of personality functioning.* Retrieved May 5, 2012, from http://www.dsm5.org/ProposedRevisions/pages/proposedrevision.aspx?rid=468.

American Psychiatric Association. (2012c). *Personality disorders.* Retrieved June 1, 2012, from http://www.dsm5.org/proposedrevision/Pages/PersonalityDisorders.aspx.

American Psychiatric Association. (2012d). *Rationale for the proposed changes to the personality disorders classification in DSM-5.* Retrieved May 5, 2012, from http://www.dsm5.org/Documents/Personality%20Disorders/Rationale%20for%20the%20Proposed%20changes%20to%20the%20Personality%20Disorders%20in%20DSM-5%205-1-12.pdf.

American Psychiatric Association. (2013). *Diagnostic and Statistical Manual of Mental Disorders* (5th ed.). Arlington, VA: Author.

Bernstein, D. P., Iscan, C. & Maser, J. (2007). Opinions of personality disorder experts regarding the DSM-IV personality disorders classification system. *Journal of Personality Disorders*, *21*, 536-551. doi: 10.1521/pedi.2007.21.5.536.

Bornstein, R. F. (1998). Reconceptualizing personality disorder diagnosis in the DSM-V: The discriminant validity challenge. *Clinical Psychology: Science and Practice*, *5*, 333-343. doi: 10.1111/j.1468-2850.1998.tb00153.x.

Bornstein, R. F. (2011). Toward a multidimensional model of personality disorder diagnosis: Implications for DSM-5. *Journal of Personality Assessment*, *93*, 362-369. doi: 10.1080/00223891.2011.577474.

Butrus, N. & Witenberg, R. T. (2015). The relationships between Five-Factor Model personality traits and personality disorder features in an Australian non-clinical sample. *Journal of Psychopathology and Behavioral Assessment*, *37*, 12-26. doi: 10.1007/s10862-014-9445-y.

Chanen, A. M., Jackson, H. J., McGorry, P. D., Allot, K. A., Clarkson, V. & Yuen, H. P. (2004). Two-year stability of personality disorder in older adolescent outpatients. *Journal of Personality Disorders*, *18*, 526-541. doi: 10.1521/pedi.18.6.526.54798.

Clark, L. A. (1993). *Manual for the Schedule for Nonadaptive and Adaptive Personality*. Minneapolis, MN: University of Minnesota Press.

Clark, L. A. (2005). Temperament as a unifying basis for personality and psychopathology. *Journal of Abnormal Psychology*, *114*, 505-521. doi: 10.1037/0021-843X.114.4.505.

Clark, L. A. (2007). Assessment and diagnosis of personality disorder: Perennial issues and emerging reconceptualization. *Annual Review of Psychology*, *58*, 227-257. doi: 10.1146/annurev.psych.57.102904. 190200.

Clark, L. A. & Livesley, W. J. (2002). Two approaches to identifying the dimensions of personality disorder: Convergence on the Five-Factor Model. In P. T. Costa, Jr. & T. A. Widiger (Eds.), *Personality disorders and the Five-Factor Model of personality*, (2nd ed., pp. 161-176). Washington, DC: American Psychological Association.

Clark, L. A., Livesley, W. J., Schroeder, M. L. & Irish, S. L. (1996). Convergence of two systems for assessing specific traits of personality disorder. *Psychological Assessment*, *8*, 294-303. doi: 10.1037/1040-3590.8.3.294.

Clark, L. A., McEwen, J. L., Collard, L. M. & Hickok, L. G. (1993). Symptoms and traits of personality disorder: Two new methods for their assessment. *Psychological Assessment*, *5*, 81-91. doi: 10.1037/1040-3590.5.1.81.

Clark, L. A., Simms, L. J., Wu, K. D. & Casillas, A. (in press). *Manual for the Schedule for Nonadaptive and Adaptive Personality-2 (SNAP-2)*. Minneapolis, MN: University of Minnesota Press.

Clark, L. A., Vorhies, L. & McEwan, J. L. (2002). Personality disorder symptomology from the Five-Factor Model perspective. In P. T. Costa, Jr. & T. A. Widiger (Eds.), *Personality disorders and the Five-Factor Model of personality*, (2nd ed., pp. 125-147). Washington, DC: American Psychological Association.

Clark, L. A. & Watson, D. (1990). *General Temperament Survey*. Unpublished test. Southern Methodist University, Dallas, TX.

Clark, L. A. & Watson, D. (2008). Temperament: An organizing paradigm for trait psychology. In O. P. John, R. W. Robins & L. A. Pervin (Eds.), *Handbook of personality: Theory and research*, (3rd ed., pp. 265-286). New York: The Guilford Press.

Clark, L. A., Watson, D. & Reynolds, S. (1995). Diagnosis and classification of psychopathology: Challenges to the current system and future directions. *Annual Review of Psychology*, *46*, 121-153. doi: 10.1146/annurev.ps.46.020195.001005.

Cohen, J. (1988). *Statistical power analysis for the behavioral sciences* (2nd ed.). Hillsdale, NJ: Lawrence Erlbaum Associates.

Coid, J., Yang, M., Tyrer, P., Roberts, A. & Ullrich, S. (2006). Prevalence and correlates of personality disorder in Great Britain. *British Journal of Psychiatry*, *188*, 423-431. doi: 10.1192/bjp.188.5.423.

Fossati, A., Maffei, C., Bagnato, M., Battaglia, M., Donati, D., Donini, M. & Prolo, F. (2000). Patterns of covariation of DSM-IV personality disorders in a mixed psychiatric sample. *Comprehensive Psychiatry*, *41*, 206-215. doi: 10.1016/S0010-440X(00)90049-X.

Frances, A. J. (1993). Dimensional diagnosis of personality—not whether, but when and which. *Psychological Inquiry*, *4*, 110-111. doi: 10.1207/s15327965pli0402_7.

Gunderson, J. G. (2010). Commentary on "Personality Traits and the Classification of Mental Disorders: Toward a More Complete Integration in DSM-5 and an Empirical Model of Psychopathology". *Personality Disorders: Theory, Research, and Treatment*, *1*, 119-122. doi: 10.1037/a0019974.

Haslam, N., Holland, E. & Kuppens, P. (2012). Categories versus dimensions in personality and psychopathology: A quantitative review of taxometric research. *Psychological Medicine*, *42*, 903-920. doi: 10.1017/S0033291711001966.

Haslam, N. & Williams, B. (2006). Taxometrics. In S. Strack (Ed.), *Differentiating normal and abnormal personality*, (2nd ed., pp. 283-308). New York: Springer Publishing Company.

Hurt, S. & Oltmanns, T. F. (2002). Personality traits and pathology in older and younger incarcerated women. *Journal of Clinical Psychology*, *58*, 457-464. doi: 10.1002/jclp.1155.

Jablensky, A. (2002). The classification of personality disorders: Critical review and need for rethinking. *Psychopathology*, *35*, 112-116. doi: 10.1159/000065129.

Johnson, J. G., First, M. B., Cohen, P. & Skodol, A. E. (2005). Adverse outcomes associated with Personality Disorder Not Otherwise

Specified in a community sample. *American Journal of Psychiatry*, *162*, 1926-1932. doi: 10.1176/appi.ajp.162.10.1926.

Kotov, R., Gamez, W., Schmidt, F. & Watson, D. (2010). Linking "Big" personality traits to anxiety, depressive, and substance use disorders: A meta-analysis. *Psychological Bulletin*, *136*, 768-821. doi: 10.1037/a0020327.

Krueger, R. F., Derringer, J., Markon, K. E., Watson, D. & Skodol, A. E. (2012). Initial construction of a maladaptive personality trait model and inventory for DSM-5. *Psychological Medicine*, *42*, 1879-1890. doi: 10.1017/S0033291711002674.

Krueger, R. F., Eaton, N. R., Derringer, J., Markon, K. E., Watson, D. & Skodol, A. E. (2011). Personality in DSM-5: Helping delineate personality disorder content and framing the metastructure. *Journal of Personality Assessment*, *93*, 325-331. doi: 10.1080/00223891. 2011. 577478.

Livesley, W. J. (2001). Conceptual and taxonomic issues. In W. J. Livesley (Ed.), *Handbook of personality disorders: Theory, research, and treatment* (pp. 3-38). New York: The Guilford Press.

Livesley, W. J. (2006). The Dimensional Assessment of Personality Pathology (DAPP) approach to personality disorder. In S. Strack (Ed.), *Differentiating normal and abnormal personality*, (2nd ed., pp. 401-429). New York: Springer Publishing Company.

Loranger, A. W. (1999). *International Personality Disorder Examination: DSM-IV and ICD-10 Interviews*. Lutz, FL: Psychological Assessment Resources.

Markon, K. E., Krueger, R. F. & Watson, D. (2005). Delineating the structure of normal and abnormal personality: An integrative hierarchical approach. *Journal of Personality and Social Psychology*, *88*, 139-157. doi: 10.1037/0022-3514.88.1.139.

Miller, J. D., Maples, J., Few, L. R., Morse, J. Q., Yaggi, K. E. & Pilkonis, P. A. (2010). Using clinician-rated Five-Factor Model data to score the DSM-IV personality disorders. *Journal of Personality Assessment*, *92*, 296-305. doi: 10.1080/00223891.2010.481984.

Miller, J. D., Reynolds, S. K. & Pilkonis, P. A. (2004). The validity of the Five-Factor Model prototypes for personality disorders in two clinical samples. *Psychological Assessment*, *16*, 310-322. doi: 10.1037/1040-3590.16.3.310.

Millon, T. (2011). *Disorders of personality: Introducing a DSM/ICD spectrum from normal to abnormal* (3rd ed.). Hoboken, NJ: John Wiley & Sons.

Morey, L. C., Warner, M. B., Shea, M. T., Gunderson, J. G., Sanislow, C. A., Grilo, C. & McGlashan, T. H. (2003). The representation of four personality disorders by the Schedule for Nonadaptive and Adaptive Personality dimensional model of personality. *Psychological Assessment*, *15*, 326-332. doi: 10.1037/1040-3590.15.3.326.

Oldham, J. M. (2009). Personality disorders: Recent history and the DSM system. In J. M. Oldham, A. E. Skodol & D. S. Bender (Eds.), *Essentials of personality disorders*, (pp. 3-11). Arlington, VA: American Psychiatric Publishing.

Pfohl, B., Blum, N. & Zimmerman, M. (1997). *Structured Interview for DSM-IV Personality (SIDP-IV)*. Washington, DC: American Psychiatric Press.

Pfohl, B., Blum, N., Zimmerman, M. & Stangl, D. (1989). *Structured Interview for DSM-III-R Personality (SIDP-R)*. Iowa City, IA: University of Iowa College of Medicine.

Pincus, A. L. & Lukowitsky, M. R. (2010). Pathological narcissism and narcissistic personality disorder. *Annual Review of Clinical Psychology*, *6*, 421-446. doi: 10.1146/annurev.clinpsy.121208.131215.

Pryor, L. R., Miller, J. D. & Gaughan, E. T. (2009). Testing two alternative pathological personality measures in the assessment of psychopathy: An examination of the SNAP and DAPP-BQ. *Journal of Personality Disorders*, *23*, 85-100. doi: 10.1521/pedi.2009.23.1.85.

Reynolds, S. K. & Clark, L. A. (2001). Predicting dimensions of personality disorder from domains and facets of the Five-Factor Model. *Journal of Personality*, *69*, 199-222. doi: 10.1111/1467-6494.00142.

Ross, S. R., Lutz, C. J. & Bailley, S. E. (2004). Psychopathy and the Five-Factor Model in a noninstitutionalized sample: A domain and facet level analysis. *Journal of Psychopathology and Behavioral Assessment*, *26*, 213-223. doi: 10.1023/B:JOBA.0000045337.48535.a5.

Samuel, D. B., Simms, L. J., Clark, L. A., Livesley, W. J. & Widiger, T. A. (2010). An item response theory integration of normal and abnormal personality scales. *Personality Disorders: Theory, Research, and Treatment*, *1*, 5-21. doi: 10.1037/a0018136.

Samuel, D. B. & Widiger, T. A. (2008). A meta-analytic review of the relationships between the five-factor model and DSM-IV-TR personality disorders: A facet level analysis. *Clinical Psychology Review*, *28*, 1326-1342. doi: 10.1016/j.cpr.2008.07.002.

Samuel, D. B. & Widiger, T. A. (2010). Comparing personality disorder models: Cross-method assessment of the FFM and DSM-IV-TR. *Journal of Personality Disorders*, *24*, 721-745. doi: 10.1521/pedi.2010.24.6.721.

Samuel, D. B. & Widiger, T. A. (2011). Conscientiousness and obsessive-compulsive personality disorder. *Personality Disorders: Theory, Research, and Treatment*, *2*, 161-174. doi: 10.1037/a0021216.

Saulsman, L. M. & Page, A. C. (2004). The Five-Factor Model and personality disorder empirical literature: A meta-analytic review. *Clinical Psychology Review*, *23*, 1055-1085. doi: 10.1016/j.cpr.2002.09.001.

Schmidt, J. A., Wagner, C. C. & Kiesler, D. J. (1993). DSM-IV Axis II: Dimensionality ratings? "Yes"; Big Five? "Perhaps later". *Psychological Inquiry*, *4*, 119-121. doi: 10.1207/s15327965pli0402_11.

Simms, L. J. & Clark, L. A. (2006). The Schedule for Nonadaptive and Adaptive Personality (SNAP): A dimensional measure of traits relevant to personality and personality pathology. In S. Strack (Ed.), *Differentiating normal and abnormal personality*, (2nd ed., pp. 432-450). New York: Springer Publishing Company.

Skodol, A. E. (2009). Manifestations, clinical diagnosis, and comorbidity. In J. M. Oldham, A. E. Skodol & D. S. Bender (Eds.), *Essentials of personality disorders*, (pp. 37-61). Arlington, VA: American Psychiatric Publishing.

Skodol, A. E. (2011). Scientific issues in the revision of personality disorders for DSM-5. *Personality and Mental Health*, *5*, 97-111. doi: 10.1002/pmh.161.

Skodol, A. E., Bender, D. S., Morey, L. C., Clark, L. A., Oldham, J. M., Alarcon, R. D. & Siever, L. J. (2011). Personality disorder types proposed for DSM-5. *Journal of Personality Disorders*, *25*, 136-169. doi: 10.1521/pedi.2011.25.2.136.

Skodol, A. E., Clark, L. A., Bender, D. S., Krueger, R. F., Morey, L. C., Verheul, R. & Oldham, J. M. (2011). Proposed changes in personality and personality disorder assessment and diagnosis for DSM-5 Part I: Description and rationale. *Personality Disorders: Theory, Research, and Treatment*, *2*, 4-22. doi: 10.1037/a0021891.

Spitzer, R. L., First, M. B., Shedler, J., West, S. G. & Skodol, A. E. (2008). Clinical utility of five dimensional systems for personality disorders: A "consumer preference" study. *The Journal of Nervous and Mental Disease*, *196*, 356-374. doi: 10.1097/NMD.0b013e3181710950.

Stepp, S. D., Trull, T. J., Burr, R. M., Wolfenstein, M. & Vieth, A. Z. (2005). Incremental validity of the Structured Interview for the Five-Factor Model of personality (SIFFM). *European Journal of Personality*, *19*, 343-357. doi: 10.1002/per.565.

Tackett, J. L., Balsis, S., Oltmanns, T. F. & Krueger, R. F. (2009). A unifying perspective on personality pathology across the life span: Developmental considerations for the fifth edition of the Diagnostic and Statistical Manual of Mental Disoders. *Development and Psychopathology*, *21*, 687-713. doi: 10.1017/S095457940900039X.

Trull, T. J. & Durrett, C. A. (2005). Categorical and dimensional models of personality disorder. *Annual Review of Clinical Psychology*, *1*, 355-380. doi: 10.1146/annurev.clinpsy.1.102803.144009.

Trull, T. J. & Widiger, T. A. (1997). *Structured Interview for the Five-Factor Model of personality (SIFFM): Professional manual*. Odessa, FL: Psychological Assessment Resources.

Verheul, R., Bartak, A. & Widiger, T. A. (2007). Prevalence and construct validity of Personality Disorder Not Otherwise Specified (PDNOS). *Journal of Personality Disorders*, *21*, 359-370. doi: 10.1521/pedi.2007.21.4.359.

Verheul, R. & Widiger, T. A. (2004). A meta-analysis of the prevalence and usage of the Personality Disorder Not Otherwise Specified (PDNOS) diagnosis. *Journal of Personality Disorders*, *18*, 309-319. doi: 10.1521/pedi.18.4.309.40350.

Watson, D., Clark, L. A. & Carey, G. (1988). Positive and Negative Affectivity and their relation to anxiety and depressive disorders. *Journal of Abnormal Psychology*, *97*, 346-353. doi: 10.1037/0021-843X.97.3.346.

Watson, D., Kotov, R. & Gamez, W. (2006). Basic dimensions of temperament in relation to personality and psychopathology. In R. F. Krueger & J. L. Tackett (Eds.), *Personality and psychopathology*, (pp. 7-38). New York: Guilford Press.

Widiger, T. A. (2001). Official classification systems. In W. J. Livesley (Ed.), *Handbook of personality disorders: Theory, research, and treatment*, (pp. 60-83). New York: The Guilford Press.

Widiger, T. A. (2007). Alternatives to DSM-IV: Axis II. In W. O'Donohue, K. A. Fowler & S. O. Lilienfeld (Eds.), *Personality disorders: Toward the DSM-V*, (pp. 21-40). Thousand Oaks, CA: SAGE Publications.

Widiger, T. A., Costa, P. T. Jr. & McCrae, R. R. (2002). A proposal for Axis II: Diagnosing personality disorders using the Five-Factor Model. In P. T. Costa, Jr. & T. A. Widiger (Eds.), *Personality disorders and the Five-Factor Model of personality*, (2nd ed., pp. 431-456). Washington, DC: American Psychological Association.

Widiger, T. A. & Frances, A. J. (2002). Toward a dimensional model for the personality disorders. In P. T. Costa, Jr. & T. A. Widiger (Eds.), *Personality disorders and the Five-Factor Model of personality*, (2nd ed., pp. 23-44). Washington, DC: American Psychological Association.

Widiger, T. A., Livesley, W. J. & Clark, L. A. (2009). An integrative dimensional classification of personality disorder. *Psychological Assessment*, *21*, 243-255. doi: 10.1037/a0016606.

Widiger, T. A. & Mullins-Sweatt, S. N. (2009). Five-Factor Model of personality disorder: A proposal for DSM-V. *Annual Review of Clinical Psychology*, *5*, 197-220. doi: 10.1146/annurev.clinpsy. 032408.153542.

Widiger, T. A. & Samuel, D. B. (2005). Diagnostic categories or dimensions? A question for the Diagnostic and Statistical Manual of Mental Disorders-Fifth Edition. *Journal of Abnormal Psychology*, *114*, 494-504. doi: 10.1037/0021-843X.114.4.494.

Widiger, T. A. & Simonsen, E. (2005). Alternative dimensional models of personality disorder: Finding a common ground. *Journal of Personality Disorders*, *19*, 110-130. doi: 10.1521/pedi.19.2.110.62628.

Widiger, T. A. & Trull, T. J. (2007). Plate tectonics in the classification of personality disorder: Shifting to a dimensional model. *American Psychologist*, *62*, 71-83. doi: 10.1037/0003-066X.62.2.71.

Widiger, T. A., Trull, T. J., Clarkin, J. F., Sanderson, C. & Costa, P. T. Jr. (1994). A description of the DSM-III-R and DSM-IV personality disorders with the Five-Factor Model of personality. In P. T. Costa, Jr. & T. A. Widiger (Eds.), *Personality disorders and the Five-Factor Model of personality*, (pp. 41-56). Washington, DC: American Psychological Association.

Wolf, E. J., Harrington, K. M. & Miller, M. W. (2011). Psychometric properties of the Schedule for Nonadaptive and Adaptive Personality in a PTSD sample. *Psychological Assessment*, *23*, 911-924. doi: 10.1037/a0023985.

World Health Organization. (1992). *International Statistical Classification of Diseases and Related Health Problems*, (10th ed. Vol. *2*). Geneva: Author.

Wright, A. G. C. (2011). Qualitative and quantitative distinctions in personality disorder. *Journal of Personality Assessment*, *93*, 370-379. doi: 10.1080/00223891.2011.577477.

Zanarini, M. C., Frankenberg, F. R., Sickel, A. E. & Yong, L. (1996). *The Diagnostic Interview for DSM-IV Personality Disorders (DIPD-IV)*. Belmont, MA: McLean Hospital.

Zimmerman, M. (2012). Is there adequate empirical justification for radically revising the personality disorders section for DSM-5? *Personality Disorders: Theory, Research, and Treatment*, *3*, 444-457. doi: 10.1037/a0022108.

Zimmerman, M., Rothschild, L. & Chelminski, I. (2005). The prevalence of DSM-IV personality disorders in psychiatric outpatients. *American Journal of Psychiatry*, *162*, 1911-1918. doi: 10.1176/appi.ajp. 162.10.1911.

About the Author

Ninawa Butrus (MPsych/PhD in Clinical Psychology, Australian Catholic University) is a Clinical Psychologist in private practice based in Melbourne, Australia. She has expertise in the psychological assessment and treatment of personality disorders and violent behaviour. Her personality research focuses on individual differences in normal and abnormal personality variation, and their respective correlates, and on dimensional models of personality pathology. She has presented her research at national and international conferences and has authored papers that have been published in book chapters and peer-reviewed academic journals.

In: Personality Disorders
Editors: Levi I. Truslow et al.
ISBN: 978-1-53615-139-8
© 2019 Nova Science Publishers, Inc.

Chapter 2

TWO METHODS FOR OPERATIONALIZING THE INTERPERSONAL SITUATION TO INVESTIGATE PERSONALITY PATHOLOGY AND INTERPERSONAL PERCEPTION IN DAILY LIFE

Emily A. Dowgwillo[1,*], Aaron L. Pincus, Michelle G. Newman, Stephen J. Wilson[1], Peter C. M. Molenaar[2] and Kenneth N. Levy[2]

[1]Department of Psychology, Pennsylvania State University, University Park, PA, US

[2] Department of Human Development and Family Studies, Pennsylvania State University, University Park, PA, US

ABSTRACT

Although contemporary conceptualizations of personality pathology define it as a disorder of perceiving self and others and relating self to others, research on the effects of interpersonal perception in personality

[*] Corresponding Author Email: ead205@psu.edu.

disorders is limited. Utilizing the interpersonal situation framework, this chapter presents two analytic methods for investigating the associations between patients' interpersonal perception and their symptom expression, emotions, and functioning in daily life. Psychotherapy outpatients (N = 57) used smartphones to complete event-contingent surveys assessing perceptions of self and other, emotional states, symptoms, and functioning after every face-to-face social interaction lasting more than 3 minutes over the course of 21 days. The first approach to the data employs multilevel modeling analyses to examine severity of personality impairment as a moderator of associations between interpersonal perception and psychological state. These findings help to move the field of personality pathology beyond cross-sectional description and classification by providing information on dynamic patient functioning in daily life. However, these inferences can only be applied to populations as a whole and may not apply to specific individuals. The second approach to the data extends these findings by applying person specific analyses to describe the interpersonal dynamics for three individual patients from the sample. Examining how interpersonal perception relates to psychological states for specific individuals demonstrates the efficacy and utility of a person specific analytic approach and illustrates how findings at the person level can and do differ from findings at the population level. We discuss the implications for understanding personality pathology from an interpersonal perspective and suggest future directions using these methods.

INTRODUCTION

This chapter briefly reviews what we know about the categorical approach to classifying personality disorders found in Section II of the *Diagnostic and Statistical Manual of Mental Disorders—5th Edition* (DSM-5; American Psychological Association, 2013) and the hybrid approach associated with the Alternative Model for Personality Disorders (AMPD; Skodol, 2012; Zachar, Krueger, & Kendler, 2015) found in Section III of the DSM-5. We suggest that future research employ the interpersonal situation framework (Pincus, Hopwood, & Wright, in press) and focus on validating and revising the AMPD in order to support it as a replacement for the outdated categorical system in subsequent revisions of the DSM. We then present an example of this research. Specifically, we examine dynamic interpersonal processes associated with the etiology and maintenance of personality impairment using an experience sampling methodology and two different data analytic approaches to quantify how patients' perceptions of self and other influence their symptom expression, emotions, and functioning in daily life.

Categorical Classification of Personality Disorders

Personality disorders are a form of psychopathology arising from impairments in self- and relational functioning. Although personality disorder symptoms contribute to a wide variety of urgent secondary complaints including anxiety, depression, disordered eating, self-harm, substance abuse, suicidality, aggression and others, it is problems with core identity (self) and maladaptive social behavior (other) that distinguish personality disorders from other kinds of psychopathology.

The classification of personality disorders began in the first half of the 20th century. Personality disorders were identified and discussed in Freud's (1914) psychoanalytic theory, Reich's (1949) character analysis, and other early psychodynamic formulations. By the 1950's, a categorical classification of personality disorders emerged in descriptive psychiatry (Schneider, 1950), and this approach continued with the classification of personality disorders found in the *Diagnostic and Statistical Manual of Mental Disorders—3rd Edition* (*DSM-III*; American Psychiatric Association, 1980; Decker, 2013) and its subsequent revisions.

Historically, the DSM has classified the various personality disorders as distinct categories, including schizoid, paranoid, schizotypal, histrionic, borderline, narcissistic, antisocial, obsessive-compulsive, dependent, and avoidant personality disorders. For the last 20 years, the accumulated criticisms of this categorical approach have undermined its construct validity and clinical utility. These criticisms have included: i) high rates of comorbidity, ii) large within-diagnosis heterogeneity due to polythetic diagnostic algorithms, iii) arbitrary diagnostic thresholds, iv) high prevalence of the Personality Disorder—Not Otherwise Specified diagnosis, v) diagnostic criteria that lack fidelity to clinical constructs, vi) taxometric analyses that favor dimensions over categories, and vii) the lack of empirically developed treatments for most categorical diagnoses (e.g., Clark, Livesley, & Morey, 1997; Haslam, Holland, & Kuppens, 2012; Hopwood, 2018b; Pincus, 2011; Verheul & Widiger, 2004; Widiger & Samuel, 2005).

At the beginning of the revision process for DSM-5, a neurobiological and genetic paradigm shift was taking hold in the study of psychopathology. As a result, major changes in the basis for classification and diagnosis were expected at the outset of the revision process. These lofty aims can be traced back to the monograph *A Research Agenda for DSM-V* (Kupfer, First, & Reiger, 2002). Eleven conferences took place over several years to review concepts, research, and proposals, but by the time the revision was due (and needed), the science had not yet caught up with the field's ambitions. With the exceptions of moving some disorders around and discontinuing the multiaxial format, the ultimate revisions were more modest. Nowhere is this more evident than for the personality disorders. In fact, the DSM-5 contains 2 independent diagnostic systems for personality disorders. The main "Section II" diagnostic chapter simply reprints the categorical DSM-IV (American Psychiatric Association, 1994) diagnostic criteria. This is unfortunate as it ignores years of research highlighting the limitations of the categorical classification of personality disorders, and an even more abundant research literature indicating that individual differences in personality and its pathology are best assessed and understood using dimensional trait models (Widiger & Simonsen, 2005). Luckily, the Alternative Model for Personality Disorders (AMPD), developed as part of the revision process, was included in DSM-5 Section III to encourage future research on the model. The hope is that with more research this model will help psychology and psychiatry shift to a more empirically supported and clinically useful classification of personality pathology (Kreuger, 2013; Pincus, 2013).

THE DSM-5 ALTERNATIVE MODEL FOR PERSONALITY DISORDERS

During the revision process, the Personality and Personality Disorder Work Group (PPDWG) examined complex and competing proposals for a new diagnostic system and considered important diagnostic issues such as the usefulness of prototype versus dimensional diagnosis and the evidential value of clinical experience versus empirical data. The PPDWG concluded a hybrid approach to personality disorder diagnosis (Krueger, Skodol, Livesley, Shrout, & Huang, 2007) could enhance acceptance of a new model by striking a balance between introducing dimensional elements, which have substantial empirical support (Kreuger & Markon, 2014; Widiger & Trull, 2007), while preserving continuity with legacy DSM categories with demonstrated clinical traction.

According to the AMPD model, diagnosis requires fulfilling 7 general criteria for personality disorder. Most innovative are the first two criteria, Criterion A (level of personality functioning) and Criterion B (maladaptive personality traits). Criterion A involves the assessment of disturbance in self functioning (identity and self-direction) and interpersonal functioning (empathy and intimacy). Criterion B involves the assessment of pathological personality traits, which are organized into 5 broad trait domains composed of 25 specific trait facets. Criteria C through G cover issues of pervasiveness, stability, early emergence, discrimination from other mental disorders, effects of substances, and developmental stage or sociocultural environment. Table 1 depicts a schematic of Criteria A and B (see the DSM–5 website for full descriptions and available assessment instruments: http://www.psychiatry.org/psychiatrists/practice/dsm/dsm-5/online-assessment-measures).

The AMPD also permits diagnosis of six specific legacy categories of personality disorder through algorithms that combine maladaptive trait elevations with specific forms of Criterion A dysfunction. These six legacy categories include Antisocial, Avoidant, Borderline, Narcissistic, Obsessive-Compulsive, and Schizotypal personality disorders (these were chosen for inclusion on the bases of empirical support and clinical relevance, and their diagnostic algorithms were calibrated with known prevalence rates of the personality disorders). For example, Antisocial Personality Disorder can be viewed as dysfunctional behavior related to a combination of pathological trait dimensions, including manipulativeness, callousness, deceitfulness, hostility, risk taking, impulsivity, and irresponsibility. Maladaptive personality patterns not covered by these algorithms (such as paranoid, schizoid, histrionic, and dependent) are diagnosed as Personality Disorder-Trait Specified (PD-TS). A PD-TS diagnosis provides specific clinically significant trait elevations in lieu of an over-arching legacy category (e.g., PD-TS with suspiciousness, restricted affectivity, and hostility may diagnose "paranoid" personality disorder). This aims to correct the problem of the ambiguous and ubiquitous "PD Not Otherwise Specified" diagnosis by providing a scheme for clearly characterizing the numerous patients who do not fit well into existing personality disorder categories. In a related manner, additional significant trait elevations can be included with legacy categories when indicated, conveniently providing the clinician with information about patient personalities not captured by the specific personality disorder legacy category.

Ultimately, the DSM-5 Task Force approved the AMPD, but the Board of Trustees of the American Psychiatric Association rejected it and retained the traditional categorical approach (the DSM-IV personality disorders) in Section II. The AMPD is an official alternative and a recognized competitor to the traditional categorical model. It legitimately complements the DSM-5 Section II personality disorder diagnoses and has practical relevance for clinicians (Hopwood, 2018a; Waugh et al., 2017). Indeed, the DSM-5 allows for formal coding of the AMPD through use of the DSM-5 code Other Specified Personality Disorder (301.89). For the remainder of this chapter, we focus on Criterion A of the AMPD and its conceptualization of personality pathology as impairments in self and interpersonal functioning.

Table 1. Schematic of the DSM-5 Alternative Model for Personality Disorders Criteria A & Criteria B

Criteria A: Level of Personality Functioning Scale (LPFS)			
Self		Interpersonal	
(1) Identity	(2) Self-Direction	(1) Empathy	(2) Intimacy
Criteria B: Maladaptive Trait Domains (broad) and Facets (narrow)			
Negative Affectivity:	*Emotional Lability, Anxiousness, Separation Insecurity,* Submissiveness, Hostility, Perseveration, Depressivity, Suspiciousness, Restricted Affectivity		
Detachment:	*Withdrawal, Intimacy Avoidance, Anhedonia,*		
	Depressivity, Restricted Affectivity, Suspiciousness		
Antagonism:	*Manipulativenss, Deceitfulness, Grandiosity,*		
	Attention Seeking, Callousness, Hostility		
Disinhibition:	*Irresponsibility, Impulsivity, Distractibility,*		
	Risk Taking, Rigid Perfectionism		
Psychoticism:	*Unusual Beliefs and Experiences, Perceptual Dysregulation, Eccentricity*		

Note: Moderate impairment is required for diagnosis of Criteria A, defined as > 2 or more component ratings of > 2 on a 0-4 point scale. Criteria B consists of 5 Trait Domains (bolded) and 25 Trait Facets. *Italicized* facets reflect the strongest loading traits, which are used to derive domain scores. Domains may be rated globally or facets may be rated individually on a 0-3 scale. Overlap of facets on more than one domain occurs because psychopathological personality dimensions do not show simple structure (see Krueger & Markon, 2014). Definitions, assessment materials, and further details are available from the DSM-5 website: http://www.psychiatry.org/psychiatrists/practice/dsm/dsm-5/online-assessment-measures.

An Interpersonal Perspective on Criteria A of the DSM-5 AMPD

DSM-5 AMPD Criterion A defines personality pathology in terms of impairments in "self" (identity, self-direction) and "interpersonal" (empathy, intimacy) functioning. In this vein, the criterion involves how individuals think and feel about the self and others and how the self relates to others (Bender, Morey, & Skodol, 2011; Morey et al., 2011). These impairments are articulated as a set of dynamic regulatory and relational processes stratified from "no impairment" to "extreme impairment" using the Level of Personality Functioning Scale (LPFS; APA, 2013). Although AMPD Criterion A semantics differentiate self and interpersonal impairments, the two are intertwined in the LPFS diagnostic criteria (e.g., *Depends excessively on others for identity, self-esteem, and emotion regulation with compromised boundaries; Hyper-attuned to others, but only with respect to perceived relevance to self*) and the LPFS rightly renders a single severity rating. Thus, AMPD Criterion A implies that the core impairments shared by all personality disorders are interpersonal in nature (Dowgwillo, Roche, & Pincus, in press; Pincus, 2011, 2018).

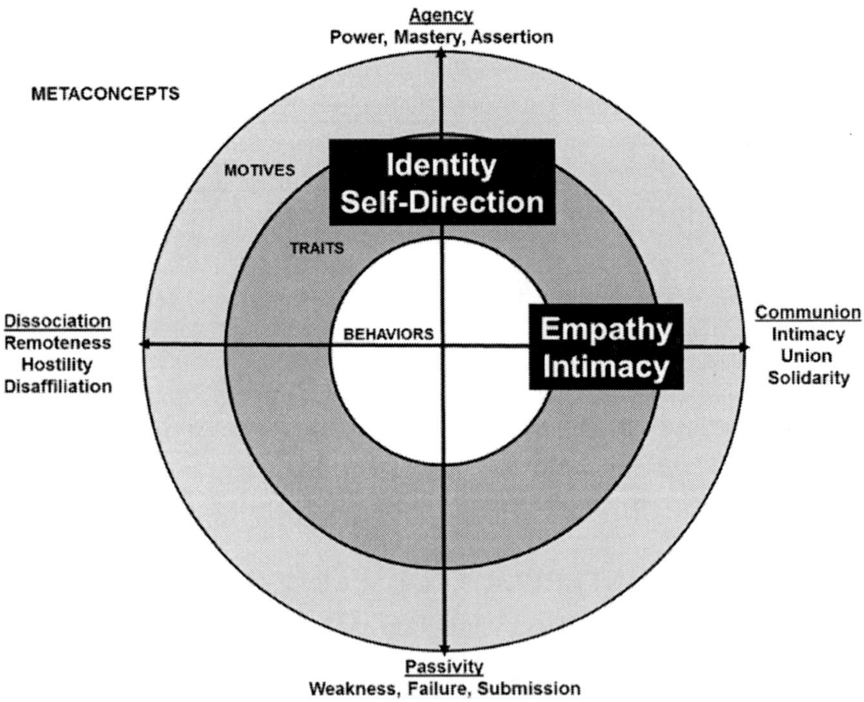

Figure 1. DSM-5 Alternative Model for Personality Disorders Criteria A aligned with the interpersonal circumplex. From Pincus, A.L. (2011). Some comments on nomology, diagnostic process, and narcissistic personality disorder in the DSM-5 proposal for personality and personality disorders. *Personality Disorders: Theory, Research, and Treatment, 2,* p. 45. Adapted with permission of the American Psychological Association.

Given this interpersonal focus, aligning the AMPD with the integrative, clinically rich, evidence-based contemporary interpersonal model of personality disorders (Pincus, 2005; Pincus & Hopwood, 2012) would i) enhance its theoretical coherence, ii) provide a mature clinical paradigm to frame empirical investigation of its components, and iii) maximize its clinical utility (Hopwood, Wright, Ansell, & Pincus, 2013; Pincus & Roche, in press; Waugh et al., 2017). This chapter focuses on these propositions by highlighting advances in interpersonal theory and assessment, reviewing recent experience sampling research on interpersonal functioning in personality disorders, and presenting an exemplary experience sampling study examining patients' perceptions of self and other, symptom expression, emotions, and functioning in daily life.

According to contemporary interpersonal theory, agency and communion are the two core metaconstructs that underlie interpersonal experience. Together, agency and communion form a superordinate structure referred to as the Interpersonal Circumplex (IPC; Wiggins, 1991, 1996), which is used to derive explanatory and descriptive concepts at different levels of specificity (e.g., motives, dispositions, behaviors). Pincus (2011) has asserted that the Criterion A impairments in self (identity, self-direction) and interpersonal (empathy, intimacy) domains align themselves with agency and communion respectively (Figure 1). Contemporary interpersonal theory combines this empirically validated structure of interpersonal functioning with empirically supported developmental, motivational, and behavioral processes to fully articulate normal and pathological personality (Pincus & Ansell, 2013). Thus, cross-sectional alignment of Criterion A impairments with agentic and communal functioning is an insufficient framework for operationalizing personality pathology (Dowgwillo et al., in press), which requires incorporation of temporally dynamic and contextualized etiological processes and maintenance mechanisms (Hopwood; Zimmermann, Pincus, & Krueger, 2015). This insufficiency is addressed by two recent advances in interpersonal theory: the evolution of the "interpersonal situation" framework for the study of personality, psychopathology, and psychotherapy (Hopwood, 2018b; Hopwood, Pincus, & Wright, in press; Pincus, Hopwood, & Wright, 2015; Pincus et al., in press), and the development of the contemporary interpersonal model of personality pathology (Pincus, 2005; Pincus & Hopwood, 2012).

The Interpersonal Situation

The interpersonal situation framework integrates the structural and process assumptions of interpersonal theory (Dawood, Dowgwillo, Wu, & Pincus, 2018; Pincus & Wright, 2011). Specifically, i) interpersonal situations involve two or more people (proximal or mentally represented) and are among the strongest situations we experience in life, and ii) the important psychological characteristics of interpersonal situations are the perceptions of agentic (dominant-submissive) and communal (nurturant-cold) motives and behaviors of self and other within and across social interactions. Figure 2 presents this framework for conceptualizing and investigating the regulatory and relational impairments of AMPD Criterion A. Both self and other are depicted and both include their own self and affect systems. The self system is organized by underlying agentic and communal interpersonal motives that lead to behavioral styles, aversions, problems, and capabilities via social learning. Identity, self-concept, and self-worth vary according to the degree to which interpersonal motives are satisfied. The affect system, which is structured by affective arousal and valence has a dynamic relationship with the self-system that is indicated by the bidirectional arrows between the interpersonal and affective circles within the self and the other. For instance, emotional experiences provide critical feedback regarding motive frustration and satisfaction that can color and intensify or dull interpersonal behavior. In turn, interpersonal behavior modulates affective experiences via the achievement of interpersonal goals and satisfaction of interpersonal motives.

The interpersonal field encapsulates the relationship between the self and other and is the arena for social exchange. Each person's perceptions of self (curved arrows) and other (unidirectional arrows) are represented as inputs, perceived in terms of their agentic and communal behaviors and impacts. The specific behaviors enacted within the field, also organized in terms of agentic (dominant-submissive) and communal (nurturant-cold) qualities, are indicated by the bidirectional arrow between self and other and simultaneously serve as input and output. Within the interpersonal field, perceptual processes moderate the functioning of the self system, affect system, and behavior. In this way, the interpersonal situation framework operationalizes regulatory and relational processes associated with personality pathology.

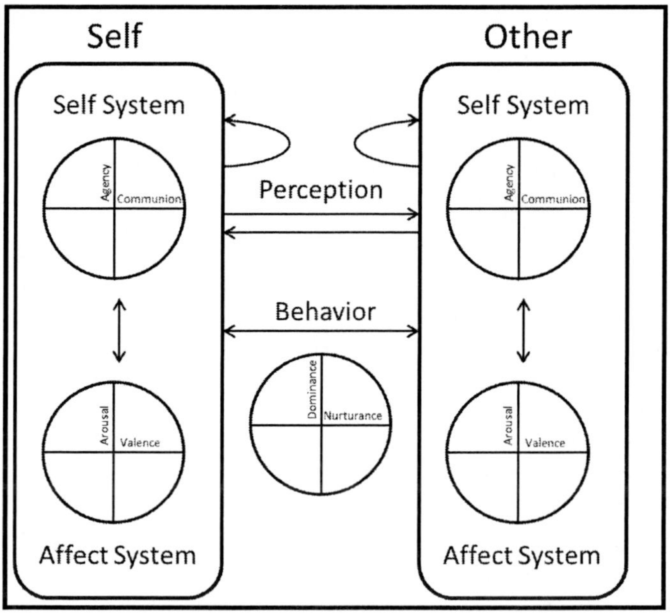

Figure 2. The interpersonal situation.

Contemporary Interpersonal Model of Personality Pathology

Interpersonal theory understands normal and disturbed interpersonal functioning in terms of the level and pervasiveness of distortion and dysregulation in interpersonal situations (Pincus, 2005; Pincus & Hopwood, 2012). Dysfunctional interpersonal styles are characterized by consistent *relational patterns of perception and regulation*, that is, input–intermediary–output chains encompassing perception, interpretation, motivation, affect, and behavior in the interpersonal situation (Eaton, South, & Krueger, 2009; Hopwood et al., 2015; Huprich & Nelson, 2015; Pincus & Wright, in press; Wright, 2014). Several potential foci are elaborated in Figure 3. *Self regulation* involves the ability to effectively manage one's social cognition and self-concept, or how one thinks about oneself in relation to others in interpersonal situations. *Affect regulation* involves the ability to modulate one's inner emotional states and affective expression, or how one feels in interpersonal situations. *Field regulation* involves modulating the processes by which one relates to others in social transactions, or how one behaves and impacts others' behavior in interpersonal situations.

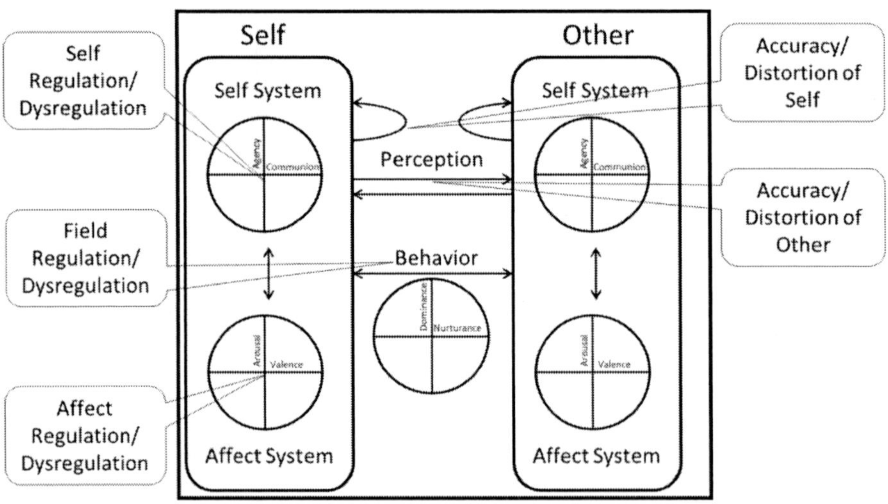

Figure 3. Dysregulation and distortion in the interpersonal situation.

To successfully navigate the social world, individuals must accurately perceive the important cues they are sending and receiving. Distortions are thought to occur when one's interpretation of the situation fits the contours of an alternative, internal, and psychologically impactful or conflictual schema that is often threatening or painful. In this sense, disturbed interpersonal relations can oftentimes be understood as a self-protective response that is consistent with a misperception deeply rooted in an individual's social learning history (Benjamin, 2003; Cain & Pincus, 2016). Table 2 creates a crosswalk between AMPD Criterion A and the contemporary interpersonal model of personality pathology.

Table 2. DSM-5 Alternative Model for Personality Disorders Criteria A Crosswalk with Interpersonal Dysregulation and Distortion

Interpersonal Dysfunction	DSM-5 AMPD Personality Impairments
Distortion	*Identity:* Accuracy of self-appraisal and self-esteem *Self-Direction:* Ability to productively self-reflect *Empathy:* Comprehension of others' experiences *Empathy:* Understanding social causality *Empathy:* Comprehension of others' motivations
Self Dysregulation	*Identity:* Experience of oneself as unique, with boundaries between self and others *Identity:* Coherent sense of time and personal history *Identity:* Stability of self-appraisal and self-esteem *Self-Direction:* Pursuit of coherent and meaningful short-term and life goals
Field Dysregulation	*Self-Direction:* Utilization of constructive and prosocial internal standards of behavior *Empathy:* Understanding social causality *Empathy:* Tolerance of others' different perspectives
	Intimacy: Desire and capacity for closeness *Intimacy:* Deep and durable connections with others
Affect Dysregulation	*Identity:* Capacity for a range of emotional experience and its regulation *Identity:* Capacity to regulate emotional experience

Studying the Interpersonal Situation and Personality Pathology

Research investigating aspects of the interpersonal situation commonly employs intensive repeated measurement of interpersonal perception and behavior using a variety of different assessment methods depending on the timescale of interest (e.g., moment-to-moment transactions, social interactions over several days or weeks) (Pincus et al., 2014; Pincus et al., in press). One common approach to examining interpersonal functioning across social interactions in daily life involves experience sampling with event contingent recording (ECR) (Moskowitz, 2009; Moskowitz & Sadikaj, 2012).

ECR designs ask participants to record their perceptions of their own and the other's agency (dominance-submission) and communion (nurturance-coldness), as well as symptoms, emotions, functioning, and contextual factors, for each face-to-face social interaction over the course of days or weeks using either paper-and-pencil or electronic surveys. Such studies generate data to examine various components of the interpersonal situation. For example, one basic question is whether individual differences in personality traits or psychopathology impact interpersonal perception and behavior. Results suggest they do. In an ECR study (Roche, Pincus, Hyde, Conroy, & Ram, 2013), individuals high in narcissism tended to see others as less communal than average whereas individuals high in dependency tended to see others as more agentic than average across social interactions. The same study also found that personality traits influenced the covariation of perceived agency and communion in predictable ways. Specifically, individuals high in dependency viewed agentic behavior by others as concurrently more communal while individuals high in narcissism viewed agentic behavior by others as concurrently less communal. Another ECR study (Russell, Moskowitz, Zuroff, Sookman, & Paris, 2007) of patients diagnosed with Borderline Personality Disorder (BPD) found they exhibited more variability in their interpersonal behavior than controls, consistent with clinical views of lability and chaotic interpersonal relations in BPD.

Research has also examined associations between personality disorders (and related pathological traits) and individual's symptoms, emotions, and functioning in relation to perceptions of self and others' interpersonal behavior. One study (Wang et al., 2014) found that the association between perceiving others as submissive and experiencing negative affect was stronger in dependent individuals compared to those low in dependency. Another study (Sadikaj, Moskowitz, & Zuroff, 2011) found the association between perceiving others as less friendly and negative affect was stronger for individuals higher on attachment anxiety and was weaker for individuals higher on attachment avoidance, and these effects were more pronounced in interactions with a romantic partner than with other persons. In a study comparing BPD patients and community controls (Sadikaj, Russell, Moskowitz, & Paris, 2010), BPD patients reported a greater increase in negative affect when they perceived others as unfriendly and a smaller increase in positive affect when they perceived others as friendly. This increased negative affect contributed to increased quarrelsome behavior in patients, instigating a cycle of negative transactions (Sadikaj, Moskowitz, Russell, Zuroff, & Paris, 2013). Similar findings linking perceived rejection with increased negative affect and aggression are reported in a study of young adult women with BPD symptoms and this was distinct from the pattern found for women with elevated antisocial personality disorder symptoms (Scott et al., 2017).

In addition to studies that highlight the importance of communal processes and interpersonal affiliation/disaffiliation for BPD, other studies demonstrate the importance of agentic processes for individuals high in narcissism. In one ECR study (Roche, Pincus, Conroy, Hyde, & Ram, 2013), individuals high in narcissism were more likely than those low in narcissism to respond to perceptions of others' dominance (a status threat) with increased dominant behavior. Relatedly, another ECR study (Wright et al., 2017) found that narcissistic personality disorder (NPD) features amplified negative affect in response to perceptions of others as dominant, which in turn predicted the patient's own quarrelsome behavior (i.e., a moderated mediation effect). Unlike BPD, NPD features were not associated with affective responses to perceptions of others' communal behavior.

So far, most ECR studies of the interpersonal situation in personality pathology focus on specific categorical personality disorder diagnoses (e.g., BPD, NPD) or specific pathological traits (e.g., dependency, narcissism, anxious attachment) using multilevel modeling to examine general associations among elements of the interpersonal situation. Such studies characterize the "typical" participant over time. Given the emergence of the DSM-5 AMPD and its distinctive partitioning of general personality pathology into self and interpersonal impairments (Criteria A) and individual differences in pathological personality traits (Criteria B), we extend the existing research in two ways using data from an ECR study of psychotherapy outpatients' social interactions over 21 days.

The first approach to the data employs multilevel modeling to initially explore associations between interpersonal perception and symptoms, emotions, and functioning. This is followed by an examination of severity of personality impairment as a moderator of these associations. These analyses help to move research on the DSM-5 AMPD beyond cross sectional associations with interpersonal dispositions (e.g., Dowgwillo et al., in press; Wright et al., 2012) by providing information on dynamic patient functioning in daily life. This intensive repeated measures approach exhibits good fidelity with Criterion A, which conceptualizes personality impairments in terms of dynamic regulatory and relational processes. However, inferences drawn from multilevel modeling can only be applied to populations as a whole and may not apply to specific individuals (Molenaar, 2004, 2013; Ram, Brinberg, Pincus, & Conroy, 2017). Fortunately, ECR data can also be analyzed at the person-specific level (Roche, Pincus, Rebar, Conroy, & Ram, 2014; Taurob et al., 2017; Yang et al., 2018). For example, when applied to a sample of BPD patients, unique linkages among the components of the interpersonal situation (perceptions of self and other, affect) emerged for individual cases (Wright et al., 2016). Thus, our second approach to the data extends findings from multilevel modeling by applying person specific analyses (Molenaar & Campbell, 2009) to describe the interpersonal dynamics for three individual patients from the sample. Examining how interpersonal perception relates to psychological states for specific individuals demonstrates the efficacy and utility of a person specific analytic approach and illustrates how findings at the person level can and do differ from findings at the population level. Finally, both analytic approaches focus on the same key components of interpersonal perception of self and other, symptoms, emotions, and functioning, providing further evidence for the validity and utility of the interpersonal situation framework for investigating personality pathology.

Two Methods for Operationalizing the Interpersonal Situation to Investigate Personality Pathology and Interpersonal Perception in Daily Life

The current study analyzes ECR data using two distinct statistical approaches to examine the relationship between interpersonal perception and symptoms, emotions, and functioning at both the population level and at the person specific level. At the population level, it is hypothesized that perceptions of agency and communion will be associated with psychological states in a sample of clinical patients and that severity of personality impairment will moderate these relationships. In particular, we predict that those with greater personality impairment will experience more symptoms, more negative affect, and poorer functioning after social interactions where they perceive others to be more agentic and less communal in general and when they perceive others to be more agentic and less communal than they usually do. At the person specific level, we hypothesize that the relationships between interpersonal perception and symptoms, emotions, and functioning will vary across individuals and will not simply replicate findings at the population level.

Method

Participants

Participants were 57 clinic outpatients recruited from a local community mental health center at intake. Eligible participants were required to receive either an anxiety disorder (N = 19) or a borderline personality disorder (N = 38) diagnosis. Patients were excluded from the study if they had a history of schizophrenia, schizoaffective disorder, bipolar I disorder, delusional disorder, delirium, dementia, amnestic disorder, cognitive disorder NOS, or active substance dependence.

Additionally, three participants who reported on a large number of social interactions were selected from this sample for person specific data analysis. Patient A is a 28 year old, female patient with BPD. She reported on 191 social interactions (7-13 interactions per day) over the course of the study. Patient B is a 46 year old, female patient with BPD. She reported on 196 interactions (5-13 interactions per day) over the course of the study. Patient C is a 22 year old, female patient with a Post Traumatic Stress Disorder (PTSD) diagnosis. She reported on 139 interactions (3-10 interactions per day) over the course of the study. All three patients were recruited at intake as part of the larger study.

Measures

Measures were administered either as part of the baseline assessment or the event contingent assessment. The baseline assessment measure was completed on the first of the 21 days during an initial training appointment. The event contingent assessments were completed each time the participant had a social interaction that lasted more than 3 minutes in duration over the course of 21 days.

Baseline Assessment. The Personality Level Measure (PLM; Morey et al., 2011) is a 64-item self-report questionnaire assessing self (identity and self direction) and interpersonal (empathy and intimacy) functioning as defined by Criterion A of the AMPD. Sample items include *I drift through life without a clear sense of direction* and *People tell me that I change so much that it sometimes seems as if I am another person.* Items are assessed using a 4-point scale ranging from 1 (Strongly Disagree) to 4 (Strongly Agree). In the current study, the PLM demonstrated high internal consistency ($\alpha = .97$).

Event Contingent Assessment. The event contingent survey items used in the current study were administered were part of a larger survey that was completed each time the participant had an interpersonal interaction that lasted more than 3 minutes. The event contingent survey was installed on a Motorola Razr smartphone with an Android operating system. Survey items asked the participant to rate how dominant (agentic) and friendly (communal) they perceived their interaction partner and themselves to be, their current levels of stress, self-esteem, anxiety, and depression (symptom ratings), their current feelings of happiness, sadness, irritability, anger, fear, and calmness (emotion ratings), and their ability to do important tasks and relate to others (functioning ratings). Responses to this subset of questions were recorded using touch point continuums ranging from 0 to 100.

Procedure

Prior to their participation, patients attended a 90-minute training session where they were introduced to the study smartphone and the procedures. They were then asked to complete ECR surveys over the next 21 days. Data were submitted electronically over a secure network and monitored daily for compliance to protocols. After 21 days, patients returned the smartphone and were compensated for the initial training session and given a prorated amount for each day of study participation.

Data Preparation and Analyses

Multilevel Modeling

Intensive repeated measures designs like the one employed here provide opportunities to examine both within-person and between person variance, but violate the assumption of independence typically employed in both correlational and regression analyses. Due to the nested data structure, using multilevel modeling allows both within and between person associations to be modeled while accommodating for the dependencies in the data (Bryk & Raudenbush, 1992). In the current study, multilevel modeling was employed to obtain estimates of the within person associations between interpersonal variables (agentic and communal perception of self and other) and psychological states (symptoms, emotions, and functioning). Additionally, we examined how severity of personality impairment moderates these associations. Responses from the event contingent survey (interpersonal perception, symptoms, emotions, and functioning ratings) comprise the Level 1 (social interaction level) data for the multilevel model, while scores on the PLM comprise the Level 2 (person level) data. Level 1 variables were centered around each person's mean score on the item across the 21 days, allowing for the clear estimation of the pooled within group slopes. This information is important in the examination of the cross level interaction between severity of personality impairment and interpersonal perception (Hofmann & Gavin, 1998).

To establish the proportion of variance in symptoms, emotions, and functioning variables attributable to individual differences, we first calculated the intraclass correlation (ICC) for each of the symptom, emotion, and functioning variables. The ICC is interpreted as the proportion of the total variance accounted for at the between person level. We then ran models to examine whether agentic and communal interpersonal perception of self and other predicted psychological state using the following general equation:

Level 1: $\text{Psychological State}_{ij} = \beta_{0i} + \beta_{1i}(\text{Within Person Interpersonal Variable}_i) + \varepsilon_{ij}$

Level 2: $\beta_{0j} = \gamma_{00} + \Upsilon_{01}(\text{iMean Interpersonal Variable}_j) + u_{0j}$

$\beta_{1j} = \gamma_{10} + u_{1j}$

where at Level 1, Psychological State_{ij} reflects each symptom/ emotion/functioning rating for individual *j* after interaction *i*, β_{0i} is a random coefficient for the intercept, β_{1i} is a random slope coefficient, and ε_{ij} represents the Level 1 residual, accounting for remaining variability in symptoms/emotions/functioning post-interaction. At Level 2, γ_{00} reflects the level 2 intercept, γ_{01} is the cross level main effect of average interpersonal perception on symptom/emotion/functioning, u_{0j} is the residual individual variability in the intercept, γ_{10} reflects the main effect of within person interpersonal perception on post interaction symptoms/emotions/functioning, and u_{1j} is the level 2 residual reflecting individual variability in this relationship.

We then examined whether severity of personality impairment as assessed by the PLM at baseline moderates the relationship between interpersonal perception and each of the symptom, emotion, and functioning variables. The following equations provide the general model structure in a multilevel format:

Level 1: Psychological $State_{ij} = \beta_{0i} + \beta_{1i}$ Within Person-Interpersonal $Variable_{i}) + \varepsilon_{ij}$

Level 2: $\beta_{0j} = \gamma_{00} + \Upsilon_{01}(PLM_j) + \Upsilon_{02}$(iMean Interpersonal $Variable_j) + \Upsilon_{03}(PLM_j$*iMean Interpersonal $Variable_j) + u_{0j}$ $\beta_{1j} = \gamma_{10} + \Upsilon_{11}(PLM_j) + u_{1j}$

where at Level 1, Psychological $State_{ij}$ reflects each symptom/emotion/ functioning rating for individual *j* after interaction *i,* β_{0i} is a random coefficient for the intercept, β_{1i} is a random slope coefficient, and ε_{ij} represents the Level 1 residual, accounting for remaining variability in symptoms/emotions/functioning post-interaction. At Level 2, γ_{00} reflects the level 2 intercept, γ_{01} is the cross level main effect of severity of personality impairment on symptoms, γ_{02} is the effect of average interpersonal perception on psychological state, γ_{03} is the between groups interaction effect of severity of personality impairment and average interpersonal perception on psychological state, u_{0j} is the residual individual variability in the intercept, γ_{10} reflects the main effect of within person interpersonal perception on symptoms/emotions/functioning, Υ_{11} reflects the cross level interaction effect of general personality severity as a moderator of the within person interpersonal perception and symptoms/emotions/functioning relationship, and u_{1j} is the level 2 residual reflecting individual variability in this relationship.

Person Specific Data Analysis

To transform the raw data into datasets with equal time intervals between measurement occasions, pchip interpolation was conducted separately for each day in MATLAB version R2015b (The Mathworks Inc., 2015). Because the participants responded to a different number of surveys each day, the number of resulting interpolated values also differed between days. To place the response times on a common metric, equally spaced response points were identified between the earliest response over the course of 21 days and the latest response over the course of 21 days. When there was no interpolated data for an identified response point, the data was considered missing. The final dataset was then treated as a 16-variate time series of length 20 for Patient A, 16 for Patient B, and 15 for Patient C (the number of observations per day) with 21 replications (the number of days). This resulted in 420, 336, and 315 measurement occasions total respectively. Results from the Augmented Dickey Fuller Test suggested that each univariate time series met the assumption of weak stationarity. A block-toeplitz covariance matrix was then created for each model to describe the intraindividual covariation of variables across successive time points (t and t + 1).

Once these block-toeplitz matrices were created, dynamic factor modeling was used to examine the relationship between interpersonal perception of self and other and psychological symptoms (Model 1), emotions (Model 2), and functioning (Model 3). The final models estimated the zero lag variance and covariance parameters among the variables at time t and the variance and covariance parameters associated with the residuals in the dynamic model. Additionally, the following regression parameters were estimated: a) each of the variables at time t predicting themselves at time t + 1, b) each the four interpersonal variables at time t predicting the psychological state variables in the model at time t + 1, and c) the psychological state variables in the model at time t predicting each of the four interpersonal variables at time t + 1. Model fitting was conducted using Lisrel, version 9.10 (Jöreskog & Sörbom, 2012). Because the sequential dependencies inherent in the data violate the assumption of independence that underlies the chi-square distribution (Molenaar, 1985), the chi square statistics was not examined to determine model fit. Instead, model fit was evaluated by examining the Standardized Root Mean Square Residual (SRMR), Root Mean Square Error of Approximation (RMSEA), Non-Normed Fit Index (NNFI), and Comparative Fit Index (CFI), indices that do not have a theoretical sampling distribution. Models were considered adequate fits to the data when three of the following four conditions were met: RMSEA ≤ 0.08, SRMR ≤ 0.1, NNFI ≥ 0.95, and CFI ≥ 0.95 (Hu & Bentler, 1999). When a model did not adequately fit, modification indices were used to iteratively free up additional regression parameters until the model exhibited adequate fit. Results from these modified models are presented in the results section.

Multilevel Modeling Results

ICCs for the psychological state variables can be found in Table 3. ICCs suggest that 49-55% of the variance in the symptom variables, 24-49% of the variance in the emotion variables, and 45-49% of the variance in the functioning variables are accounted for at the between person level. This suggests that variability in symptoms and functioning are approximately equally accounted for at the between and within person levels. However, variability in emotions, particularly happiness, sadness, irritability, and anger, seem to be attributed predominately to situational features (within person level).

Table 3. Intraclass Correlation Coefficients

	ICC
Self-Esteem	.51
Anxiety	.55
Depression	.49
Stress	.49
Happy	.24
Sad	.31
Angry	.26
Irritable	.26
Frightened	.49
Calm	.40
Ability to Do Important Tasks	.45
Ability to Relate	.49

Note. ICC = Intraclass Correlation Coefficient.

Effect of Interpersonal Perception on Psychological State

Results from the multilevel modeling analyses can be found in Table 4 through Table 7. When we examined the relationship between interpersonal perception and psychological states (Tables 4 and 5), results were consistent with our hypotheses and suggest that patients who perceived others as more agentic on average also reported experiencing greater anxiety, stress, sadness, anger, irritability, and fear during social interactions. Further, in social interactions where patients perceived the other as more agentic than they usually did, patients reported lower self-esteem, happiness, and calmness, and less ability to do important tasks and relate to others. Concurrently, the patients reported more anxiety, depression, stress, sadness, anger, irritability, and fear. Thus, perceiving dominance in others (both at the within and between person level) is generally related to increased symptom expression, increased negative emotions, decreased positive emotions, and a decreased ability to function.

Patients who tended to view themselves as more agentic on average reported experiencing greater anger, irritability, and fear during social interactions. In social interactions where they viewed themselves as more agentic than they usually did, participants reported more anger and less fear. This suggests that perceiving the self as dominant is associated with negative emotional states and may be one way that patients attempt to express anger and regulate fear.

In terms of communion, patients who tended to view either themselves or others as more communal on average reported higher self esteem, happiness, and calmness, a greater ability to do important tasks and relate to others, and lower anxiety, depression, stress, sadness, anger, and irritability in interactions. Additionally, in social interactions where patients viewed themselves or others as more communal then usual, a similar pattern of associations emerged. They also reported less fear in those interactions. Thus, perceiving nurturance in self and others (both at the within and between person level) is generally related to a greater ability to function, decreased symptom expression, increased positive emotions, and decreased negative emotions.

Personality Severity as a Moderator (Perceptions of Agency)

The results of the moderation analyses can be found in Tables 6 and 7. Severity of personality impairment significantly interacts with interpersonal perception of agency in self and others to predict symptoms, emotions, and functioning. Almost all moderation effects occurred at the between-person level. When patients with high severity of personality impairment perceive others as passive-submissive, they experience lower self-esteem, happiness, and calmness, increased stress and anxiety, and decreased ability to complete important tasks than they do when the experience others as more dominant. Patients lower in severity of personality impairment exhibited the opposite pattern (See Figure 4 for an example).

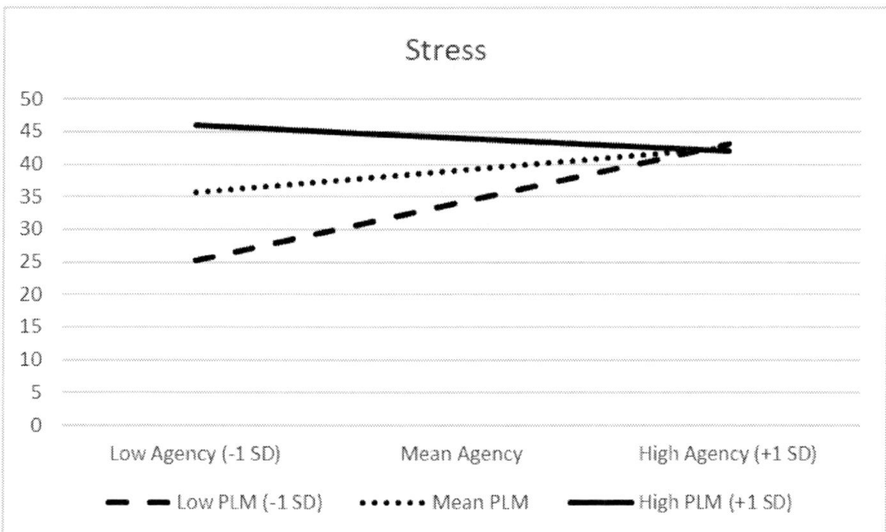

Figure 4. Severity of personality impairment (PLM score) moderates the association between interpersonal perception of others' agency and experienced stress.

Similarly, when patients with high severity of personality impairment perceive themselves as passive-submissive, they experience lower calmness and decreased ability to complete important tasks than they do when they perceive themselves as more dominant. Patients lower in severity of personality impairment exhibited the opposite pattern. Notably, the pattern of associations linked with severe personality impairments deviated from the prototypical pattern of MLM results and the pattern of associations linked with low levels of personality impairment mirrored the prototypical pattern of MLM results. One moderation effect was found at the within-person level. Patients with high severity of personality impairment reported experiencing more stress in situations where when they perceived themselves as more passive-submissive than they usually did compared to situations where they perceived themselves as less passive-submissive than they usually did. Patients with lower severity of personality impairment, exhibited the opposite pattern.

Personality Severity as a Moderator (Perceptions of Communion)

We found only one moderation effect associated with the interpersonal perception of communion, and this occurred at the within-person level. Patients with more severe personality impairment reported experiencing more depression in situations where they behaved less communally than they usually did compared to situations where they behaved more communally than they usually did. Patients with lower severity of personality impairment exhibited a similar pattern. However, these individuals reported a smaller difference in depression ratings across level of self communion compared to those with more severe personality impairment.

Discussion of MLM Results

Interpersonal perception of self and other is associated with symptom expression, emotions, and functioning in daily life. In general, perceiving communion in self and others is associated with decreased symptom expression, lower negative emotions, higher positive emotions, and increased functioning. These findings are consistent with prior research linking unfriendliness and perceived rejection with increased negative affect and aggression in studies of BPD patients (Sadikaj, Moskowitz, & Zuroff, 2011) and young women with BPD symptoms (Scott et al., 2017).

In general, perceiving agency in others is also associated with increased symptom expression, higher negative emotions, lower positive emotions, and decreased functioning. However, severity of personality impairment moderates associations between interpersonal perceptions of agency and symptoms, emotions, and functioning. For those patients with the most severe personality impairments, the opposite pattern emerges where the perception of passivity and submissiveness in self and other negatively impacts psychological states.

Given that two thirds of the patients in the current study were selected because they received a BPD diagnosis, it is interesting that agentic perceptions are more centrally associated with psychological state. These findings are inconsistent with the BPD literature linking communal perception and behavior (Sadikaj et al., 2013). Rather, they more consistent with findings typically associated with pathological narcissism and NPD (Roche et al., 2013; Wright et al., 2017). Given that the expected relationships with communion are occurring when severity is not included in the model, it is possible that using personality severity as a moderator accounts for some of the variance in psychological states that otherwise would be accounted for by communal functioning (Sharp et al., 2015). Research finding that Criterion A is cross-sectionally associated with cold (low communion) interpersonal problems (Dowgwillo et al., in press) supports this idea.

Finally, in order to empirically investigate the contemporary interpersonal model of personality pathology, we applied MLM to intensive repeated measures data collected via ECR focusing on social interactions in daily life to successfully operationalize the interpersonal situation at the population level of analysis. This allows us to describe the typical or prototypical patient but does not allow us to generalize such results to a specific patient. The following section demonstrates another approach to investigating the contemporary interpersonal model of personality pathology by operationalizing the interpersonal situation at the person-specific level of analysis.

Table 4. Effect of Interpersonal Perception on Psychological Symptoms and Functioning

	Self Esteem		**Anxiety**		**Depression**		**Stress**		**Ability to Do Important Tasks**		**Ability to Relate**	
Model 1	b	SE	b	SE	b	SE	b	SE	b	SE	b	SE
Intercept	77.92*	11.03	-3.04	13.70	2.51	10.49	6.95	12.78	81.02*	11.00	81.04*	10.66
Other Agency Mean	-.30	.20	.66*	.24	.35	.19	.55*	.23	-.36	.20	-.30	.19
Other Agency Centered	-0.12*	.03	.21*	.04	.08*	.02	.20*	.04	-.06*	.02	-.12*	.03
Model 2												
Intercept	64.79*	9.37	11.56	11.33	12.86	9.27	17.89	10.60	61.77*	9.56	71.67*	9.45
Self Agency Mean	-.07	.18	.42	.22	.17	.18	.38	.20	-.01	.18	-.14	.18
Self Agency Centered	.03	.04	.03	.04	.01	.03	.04	.04	.01	.03	.04	.03
Model 3												
Intercept	-17.63	14.89	98.72*	20.61	58.81*	17.46	105.58*	19.12	-7.10	16.05	1.44	16.38
Other Communion Mean	0.97*	.18	-.80*	.25	-.46*	.21	-.84*	.23	.84*	.19	.77*	.20
Other Communion Centered	0.36*	.04	-.31*	.04	-.21*	.03	-.34*	.04	.25*	.03	.32*	.04
Model 4												
Intercept	-9.49	14.94	77.41*	21.42	57.06*	17.46	82.16*	20.00	.85	16.40	7.45	16.20
Self Communion Mean	0.85*	.18	-.54*	.25	-.43*	.21	-.54*	.24	.73*	.19	.69*	.19
Self Communion Centered	0.41*	.04	-.34*	.04	-.23*	.04	-.37*	.04	.30*	.04	.40*	.04

Note. N = 57. SE = Standard Error. *$p<.05$.

Table 5. Effect of Interpersonal Perception on Emotions

	Happy		**Sad**		**Angry**		**Irritable**		**Frightened**		**Calm**	
Model 1	b	SE	b	SE	b	SE	b	SE	b	SE	b	SE
Intercept	73.35*	8.92	-2.47	8.68	-9.38	7.22	-1.27	8.85	-12.11	6.63	73.47*	11.37
Other Agency Mean	-.19	.16	.35*	.15	.42*	.13	.43*	.16	.39*	.12	-.30	.20
Other Agency Centered	-.25*	.05	.10*	.04	.24*	.04	.33*	.05	.06*	.02	-.21*	.04
Model 2												
Intercept	68.57*	7.19	6.74	7.04	.06	5.72	4.26	6.86	-6.32	5.75	72.30*	9.07
Self Agency Mean	-.10	.14	.19	.13	.26*	.11	.36*	.13	.31*	.11	-.30	.17
Self Agency Centered	-.01	.06	-.01	.03	.14*	.05	.10	.07	-.06*	.03	-.00	.05
Model 3												
Intercept	-5.42	10.88	51.23*	11.94	41.86*	10.22	71.48*	12.45	25.48*	10.32	-9.57	14.05
Other Communion Mean	.84*	.13	-.43*	.14	-.35*	.12	-.61*	.15	-.20	.12	.82*	.17
Other Communion Centered	.65*	.03	-.28*	.03	-.40*	.04	-.51*	.04	-.14*	.02	.43*	.04
Model 4												
Intercept	.11	10.75	42.73*	12.65	36.59*	10.64	65.46*	12.56	23.28*	11.01	11.72	13.64
Self Communion Mean	.76*	.13	-.32*	.15	-.28*	.13	-.52*	.04	-.17	.13	.55*	.16
Self Communion Centered	.69*	.04	-.30*	.04	-.47*	.04	-.60*	.15	-.15*	.03	.53*	.04

Note. N = 57. SE = Standard Error. *p<.05.

Table 6. Personality Severity as a Moderator of the Effect of Interpersonal Perception on Psychological Symptoms and Functioning

	Self Esteem		**Anxiety**		**Depression**		**Stress**		**Ability to Do Important Tasks**		**Ability to Relate**	
Model 1	b	SE	b	SE	b	SE	b	SE	b	SE	b	SE
Intercept	226.92*	53.78	-162.43*	68.66	-75.38	54.51	-147.19*	64.42	262.61*	49.49	173.43*	52.00
Severity	-1.10*	.37	1.15*	.47	.58	.37	1.10*	.44	-1.35*	.34	-.71*	.35
Other Agency Mean	-2.40*	.94	2.97*	1.20	1.36	.95	2.90*	1.13	-2.84*	.87	-1.20	.91
Other Agency Centered	-.20	.20	.36	.23	.11	.14	.33	.23	-.20	.14	-.10	.17
Severity x Other Agency Mean	.02*	.01	-.02*	.01	-.01	.01	-.02*	.01	.02*	.01	.01	.01
Severity x Other Agency Centered	.00	.00	-.00	.00	-.00	.00	-.00	.00	.00	.00	-.00	.00
Model 2												
Intercept	183.21*	48.21	-71.49	60.60	-71.77	49.90	-77.99	57.28	215.16*	45.67	168.58*	47.15
Severity	-.80*	.31	.57	.39	.57	.32	.64	.37	-1.04*	.29	-.67*	.30
Self Agency Mean	-1.65	.89	1.34	1.11	1.32	.92	1.69	1.05	-2.06*	.84	-1.14	.87
Self Agency Centered	-.09	.21	.25	.21	.24	.18	.56*	.25	-.06	.18	-.01	.20
Severity x Self Agency Mean	.01	.01	-.01	.01	-.01	.01	-.01	.01	.01*	.01	.01	.01
Severity x Self Agency Centered	.00	.00	-.00	.00	-.00	.00	-.00*	.00	.00	.00	.00	.00
Model 3												
Intercept	-28.36	107.91	149.13	148.34	-9.19	128.47	84.99	139.87	92.55	111.94	8.45	114.78
Severity	.10	.67	-.36	.92	.41	.80	.10	.87	-.58	.70	.01	.71
Other Communion Mean	1.31	1.21	-1.69	1.66	.10	1.44	-.84	1.56	.05	1.25	1.07	1.28
Other Communion Centered	.23	.22	-.12	.22	.21	.19	-.24	.23	.02	.20	.50*	.22
Severity x Other Communion Mean	-.00	.01	.01	.01	-.00	.01	.00	.01	.00	.01	-.00	.01
Severity x Other Communion Centered	.00	.00	-.00	.00	-.00*	.00	-.00	.00	.00	.00	-.00	.00
Model 4												
Intercept	11.41	111.73	84.12	160.75	-53.31	132.84	40.82	152.34	71.16	119.00	32.65	116.57
Severity	-.10	.69	-.07	.99	.67	.82	.23	.94	-.40	.73	-.12	.72
Self Communion Mean	.87	1.23	-.97	1.77	.58	1.46	-.36	1.68	.31	1.31	.80	1.28
Self Communion Centered	.23	.22	-.31	.24	.09	.23	-.42	.26	.03	.24	.46	.25
Severity x Self Communion Mean	-.00	.01	.00	.01	-.01	.01	-.00	.01	.00	.01	-.00	.01
Severity x Self Communion Centered	.00	.00	-.00	.00	-.00	.00	.00	.00	.00	.00	-.00	.00

Note. N = 57. SE = Standard Error. *p<.05.

Table 7. Personality Severity as a Moderator of the Effect of Interpersonal Perception on Emotions

	Happy		Sad		Angry		Irritable		Frightened		Calm	
Model 1	b	SE	b	SE	b	SE	b	SE	b	SE	b	SE
Intercept	174.06*	45.17	-62.39	44.14	-10.52	37.38	-80.06*	44.63	16.73	34.51	217.29*	57.38
Severity	-.73*	.31	.46	.30	.05	.25	.59*	.30	-.16	.23	-1.02*	.39
Other Agency Mean	-1.65*	.79	1.00	.77	.12	.66	1.40*	.78	-.37	.60	-2.59*	1.01
Other Agency Centered	-.44	.31	.34	.21	.38	.25	.48	.29	.16	.12	-.39	.23
Severity x Other Agency Mean	.01*	.01	-.01	.01	.00	.00	-.01	.01	.00	.00	.02*	.01
Severity x Other Agency Centered	.00	.00	-.00	.00	-.00	.00	-.00	.00	-.00	.00	.00	.00
Model 2												
Intercept	156.28*	38.17	-12.29	37.50	.58	30.41	-49.97	35.61	12.03	31.06	215.99*	46.82
Severity	-.58*	.24	.15	.24	.02	.19	.38	.23	-.10	.20	-.94*	.30
Self Agency Mean	-1.40	.70	.06	.69	-.16	.56	.86	.65	-.35	.57	-2.72*	.86
Self Agency Centered	-.31	.34	-.05	.21	.39	.28	.48	.39	.10	.17	-.02	.28
Severity x Self Agency Mean	.01	.00	.00	.00	.00	.00	-.00	.00	.00	.00	.02*	.01
Severity x Self Agency Centered	.00	.00	.00	.00	-.00	.00	-.00	.00	-.00	.00	.00	.00
Model 3												
Intercept	48.42	80.34	57.71	86.55	63.51	70.73	97.77	87.15	21.03	75.07	176.41	102.42
Severity	-.33	.50	-.06	.54	-.17	.44	-.20	.54	.01	.47	-1.16	.64
Other Communion Mean	.33	.90	-.73	.97	-.82	.79	-1.15	.97	-.35	.84	-1.19	1.14
Other Communion Centered	.91*	.19	.09	.20	-.45*	.23	-.68*	.22	.01	.15	.66*	.22
Severity x Other Communion Mean	.00	.01	.00	.01	.00	.00	.00	.01	.00	.01	.01	.01
Severity x Other Communion Centered	-.00	.00	-.00	.00	.00	.00	.00	.00	-.00	.00	-.00	.00
Model 4												
Intercept	86.13	81.81	16.57	94.86	40.79	77.27	51.89	91.45	1.39	82.92	127.40	105.83
Severity	-.53	.50	.15	.58	-.05	.48	.06	.56	.12	.51	-.72	.65
Self Communion Mean	-.07	.90	-.28	1.04	-.56	.85	-.64	1.01	-.13	.91	-.60	1.16
Self Communion Centered	.78*	.25	.04	.23	-.35	.27	-.65*	.27	.03	.18	.82*	.27
Severity x Self Communion Mean	.01	.01	.00	.01	.00	.01	.00	.01	-.00	.01	.01	.01
Severity x Self Communion Centered	-.00	.00	-.00	.00	-.00	.00	.00	.00	-.00	.00	-.00	.00

Note. N = 57. SE = Standard Error. *p<.05

Table 8. Fit Statistics for Person Specific Models

	RMSEA	SRMR	NNFI	CFI
Model 1-Symptoms				
Patient A	.00*	.02*	1.00*	1.00*
Patient B	.11	.05*	.84	.97*
Patient B (Modified)	.08*	.03*	.92	.99*
Patient C	.11	.06*	.88	.98*
Patient C (Modified)	.07*	.02*	.94	.99*
Model 2-Emotions				
Patient A	.03*	.03*	.99*	1.00*
Patient B	.11	.05*	.82	.96*
Patient B (Modified)	.08*	.03*	.91	.98*
Patient C	.10	.05*	.84	.97*
Patient C (Modified)	.08*	.05*	.91	.98*
Model 3-Functioning				
Patient A	.02*	.02*	.99*	1.00*
Patient B	.11	.05*	.81	.96*
Patient B (Modified)	.08*	.04*	.91	.98*
Patient C	.07*	.04*	.90	.98*

Note. RMSEA = Root Mean Square Error of Approximation; SRMR = Standardized Root Mean Residual; NNFI = Non-Normed Fit Index; CFI = Comparative Fit Index, * indicates that the fit statistic suggests adequate fit.

Table 9. Estimated standardized zero-lag and residual variance and covariance parameters for Model 1 (Symptoms)

Patient A								
Zero Lag								
Predictor	**Other Communion**	**Other Agency**	**Self Communion**	**Self Agency**	**Self-Esteem**	**Anxiety**	**Depression**	**Stress**
Other Communion	1.00*							
Other Agency	-.17*	1.00*						
Self Communion	.48*	-.20*	1.00*					
Self Agency	.03	-.52*	.07	1.00*				
Self-Esteem	.45*	-.14*	.43*	.12*	1.00*			
Anxiety	-.36*	.16*	-.48*	-.13*	-.49*	1.00*		
Depression	-.27*	.11*	-.21*	.06	-.42*	.24*	1.00*	
Stress	-.40*	.05	-.48*	.01	-.50*	.69*	.26*	1.00*
Residuals								
Predictor	**Other Communion**	**Other Agency**	**Self Communion**	**Self Agency**	**Self-Esteem**	**Anxiety**	**Depression**	**Stress**
Other Communion	.99*							
Other Agency	-.17*	1.00*						
Self Communion	.47*	-.20*	.97*					
Self Agency	.03	-.52*	.06	1.00*				
Self-Esteem	.45*	-.13*	.42*	.12*	.99*			
Anxiety	-.34*	.14*	-.43*	-.11*	-.46*	.92		
Depression	-.26*	.11*	-.21*	.06	-.41*	.23*	.98*	
Stress	-.39*	.05	-.47*	.00	-.50*	.67*	.25*	.98*

Table 9. (Continued)

Patient B								
Zero Lag								
Predictor	**Other Communion**	**Other Agency**	**Self Communion**	**Self Agency**	**Self-Esteem**	**Anxiety**	**Depression**	**Stress**
Other Communion	1.00*							
Other Agency	-.18*	1.00*						
Self Communion	.62*	-.30*	1.00*					
Self Agency	-.04	-.17*	.01	1.00*				
Self-Esteem	.45*	-.29*	.46*	.03	1.00*			
Anxiety	-.38*	.32*	-.38*	.07	-.47*	1.00*		
Depression	-.29*	.26*	-.29*	-.11*	-.43*	.65*	1.00*	
Stress	-.34*	.22*	-.32*	-.03	-.38*	.73*	.68*	1.00*
Residuals								
Predictor	**Other Communion**	**Other Agency**	**Self Communion**	**Self Agency**	**Self-Esteem**	**Anxiety**	**Depression**	**Stress**
Other Communion	.78*							
Other Agency	-.20*	.97*						
Self Communion	.55*	-.25*	.89*					
Self Agency	-.03	-.14*	.03	.86*				
Self-Esteem	.28*	-.34*	.40*	.04	.75*			
Anxiety	-.27*	.32*	-.33*	.01	-.39*	.91*		
Depression	-.22*	.28*	-.30*	-.09	-.39*	.64*	.98*	
Stress	-.27*	.24*	-.29*	.01	-.34*	.74*	.68*	.96*

Patient C								
Zero Lag								
Predictor	**Other Communion**	**Other Agency**	**Self Communion**	**Self Agency**	**Self-Esteem**	**Anxiety**	**Depression**	**Stress**
Other Communion	1.00*							
Other Agency	-.29*	1.00*						
Self Communion	.37*	-.13*	1.00*					
Self Agency	-.13*	.16*	-.41*	1.00*				
Self-Esteem	.65*	-.28*	.52*	-.23*	1.00*			
Anxiety	-.38*	.10	-.47*	.11	-.63*	1.00*		
Depression	-.20*	.05	-.50*	.09	-.43*	.59*	1.00*	
Stress	-.55*	.16*	-.57*	.19*	-.72*	.71*	.65*	1.00*
Residuals								
Predictor	**Other Communion**	**Other Agency**	**Self Communion**	**Self Agency**	**Self-Esteem**	**Anxiety**	**Depression**	**Stress**
Other Communion	.90*							
Other Agency	-.23*	.91*						
Self Communion	.30*	-.10	.93*					
Self Agency	-.05	.09	-.34*	.85*				
Self-Esteem	.56*	-.24*	.43*	-.17*	.87*			
Anxiety	-.32*	.06	-.38*	.05	-.50*	.85*		
Depression	-.22*	-.22*	-.47*	.09	-.38*	.50*	.86*	
Stress	-.49*	-.49*	-.48*	.12*	-.60*	.55*	.54*	.82*

Note. * indicates t>1.96, p<.05

Table 10. Estimated standardized zero-lag and residual variance and covariance parameters for Model 2 (Emotions)

Patient A										
Zero Lag										
Predictor	**Other Communion**	**Other Agency**	**Self Communion**	**Self Agency**	**Happy**	**Irritable**	**Sad**	**Frightened**	**Angry**	**Calm**
Other Communion	1.00*									
Other Agency	-.17*	1.00*								
Self Communion	.48*	-.20*	1.00*							
Self Agency	.03	-.52*	.07	1.00*						
Happy	.56*	-.22*	.60*	.06	1.00*					
Irritable	-.46*	.25*	-.64*	-.03	-.65*	1.00*				
Sad	-.29*	.11*	-.35*	-.01	-.40*	.43*	1.00*			
Frightened	-.27*	.30*	-.42*	-.16*	-.43*	.33*	.49*	1.00*		
Angry	-.50*	.22*	-.69*	-.03	-.66*	.81*	.51*	.45*	1.00*	
Calm	.43*	-.24*	.66*	.06	.62*	-.59*	-.34*	-.46*	-.63*	1.00*
Residuals										
Predictor	**Other Communion**	**Other Agency**	**Self Communion**	**Self Agency**	**Happy**	**Irritable**	**Sad**	**Frightened**	**Angry**	**Calm**
Other Communion	1.00*									
Other Agency	-.17*	.99*								
Self Communion	.48*	-.20*	1.00*							
Self Agency	.04	-.52*	.07	1.00*						
Happy	.56*	-.23*	.61*	.06	.99*					
Irritable	-.46*	.27*	-.66*	-.04	-.65*	.99*				
Sad	-.30*	.11*	-.35*	-.01	-.41*	.44*	1.00*			
Frightened	-.29*	.30*	-.42*	-.17*	-.44*	.34*	.50*	.99*		
Angry	-.50*	.22*	-.69*	-.04	-.67*	.81*	.51*	.46*	1.00*	
Calm	.43*	-.24*	.67*	.07	.62*	-.59*	-.35*	-.44*	-.63*	.97*

Patient B										
Zero Lag										
Predictor	**Other Communion**	**Other Agency**	**Self Communion**	**Self Agency**	**Happy**	**Irritable**	**Sad**	**Frightened**	**Angry**	**Calm**
Other Communion	1.00*									
Other Agency	-.18*	1.00*								
Self Communion	.62*	-.30*	1.00*							
Self Agency	-.04	-.17*	.01	1.00*						
Happy	.39*	-.24*	.40*	-.00	1.00*					
Irritable	-.52*	.37*	-.51*	.22*	-.41*	1.00*				
Sad	-.22*	.32*	-.34*	-.05*	-.15*	.53*	1.00*			
Frightened	-.09	.19*	-.01	-.14*	-.04	.20*	.27*	1.00*		
Angry	-.42*	.30*	-.37*	.29*	-.38*	.66*	.31*	.34*	1.00*	
Calm	.40*	-.28*	.35*	-.03	.54*	-.46*	-.24*	-.05	-.55*	1.00*
Residuals										
Predictor	**Other Communion**	**Other Agency**	**Self Communion**	**Self Agency**	**Happy**	**Irritable**	**Sad**	**Frightened**	**Angry**	**Calm**
Other Communion	.79*									
Other Agency	-.23*	.90*								
Self Communion	.51*	-.23*	.86*							
Self Agency	.02	-.13*	.05	.91*						
Happy	.29*	-.21*	.33*	.04	.80*					
Irritable	-.47*	.33*	-.44*	.20*	-.34*	.93*				
Sad	-.24*	.31*	-.34*	-.02	-.20*	.55*	.93*			
Frightened	-.18*	.18*	-.05	-.10*	-.16*	.20*	.31*	.87*		
Angry	-37*	.28*	-.31*	.25*	-.38*	.60*	.32*	.35*	.93*	
Calm	.29*	-.30*	.30*	.04	.38*	-.43*	-.31*	-.13*	-.53*	.85*

Table 10. (Continued)

Patient C										
Zero Lag										
Predictor	**Other Communion**	**Other Agency**	**Self Communion**	**Self Agency**	**Happy**	**Irritable**	**Sad**	**Frightened**	**Angry**	**Calm**
Other Communion	1.00*									
Other Agency	-.29*	1.00*								
Self Communion	.37*	-.13*	1.00*							
Self Agency	-.13*	.16*	-.41*	1.00*						
Happy	.49*	-.26*	.67*	-.21*	1.00*					
Irritable	-.36*	.14*	-.73*	.38*	-.69*	1.00*				
Sad	-.30*	.19*	-.05	-.13*	-.32*	.23*	1.00*			
Frightened	-.42*	.27*	-.16*	-.08	-.25*	.17*	.65*	1.00*		
Angry	-.44*	.18*	-.58*	.20*	-.61*	.69*	.48*	.53*	1.00*	
Calm	-.05	.04	-.06	.03	-.11	-.02	-.00	-.03	.07	1.00*
Residuals										
Predictor	**Other Communion**	**Other Agency**	**Self Communion**	**Self Agency**	**Happy**	**Irritable**	**Sad**	**Frightened**	**Angry**	**Calm**
Other Communion	.86*									
Other Agency	-.30*	.89*								
Self Communion	.29*	-.15*	.91*							
Self Agency	-.03	.14*	-.29*	.84*						
Happy	.35*	-.24*	.55*	-.07	.84*					
Irritable	-.32*	.14*	-.66*	.28*	-.59*	.95*				
Sad	-.34*	.17*	-.12*	-.10*	-.36*	.32*	.91*			
Frightened	-.43*	.29*	-.18*	-.07	-.25*	.21*	.64*	.99*		
Angry	-.44*	.19*	-.53*	.13*	-.55*	.66*	.55*	.55*	.95*	
Calm	-.06	.14*	-.07	.07	-.11*	-.00	-.02	-.04	.11*	.89*

Note. * indicates t>1.96, p<.05.

Table 11. Estimated standardized zero-lag and residual variance and covariance parameters for Model 3 (Functioning)

Patient A						
Zero Lag						
Predictor	**Other Communion**	**Other Agency**	**Self Communion**	**Self Agency**	**Ability to Do Important Tasks**	**Ability to Relate**
Other Communion	1.00*					
Other Agency	-.17*	1.00*				
Self Communion	.48*	-.20*	1.00*			
Self Agency	.03	-.52*	.07	1.00*		
Ability to Do Important Tasks	-.40*	.19*	-.45*	-.09	1.00*	
Ability to Relate	-.02	.19*	-.17*	-.02	.37*	1.00*
Residuals						
Predictor	**Other Communion**	**Other Agency**	**Self Communion**	**Self Agency**	**Ability to Do Important Tasks**	**Ability to Relate**
Other Communion	1.00*					
Other Agency	-.17*	.99*				
Self Communion	.48*	-.20*	1.00*			
Self Agency	.03	-.52*	.07	1.00*		
Ability to Do Important Tasks	-.40*	.18*	-.45*	-.09	.97*	
Ability to Relate	-.02	.18*	-.17*	-.02	.37*	.99*

Table 11. (Continued)

Patient B						
Zero Lag						
Predictor	**Other Communion**	**Other Agency**	**Self Communion**	**Self Agency**	**Ability to Do Important Tasks**	**Ability to Relate**
Other Communion	1.00*					
Other Agency	-.18*	1.00*				
Self Communion	.62*	-.30*	1.00*			
Self Agency	-04	-.17*	.01	1.00*		
Ability to Do Important Tasks	.32*	-.00	.29*	-.05	1.00*	
Ability to Relate	.36*	-.04	.25*	-.02	.60*	1.00*
Residuals						
Predictor	**Other Communion**	**Other Agency**	**Self Communion**	**Self Agency**	**Ability to Do Important Tasks**	**Ability to Relate**
Other Communion	.80*					
Other Agency	-.23*	.94*				
Self Communion	.54*	-.26*	.90*			
Self Agency	-.01	-.20*	.04	.96*		
Ability to Do Important Tasks	.06	-.13*	.20*	.01	.56*	
Ability to Relate	.16*	-.16*	.18*	.01	.25*	.69*

Patient C						
Zero Lag						
Predictor	**Other Communion**	**Other Agency**	**Self Communion**	**Self Agency**	**Ability to Do Important Tasks**	**Ability to Relate**
Other Communion	1.00*					
Other Agency	-.29*	1.00*				
Self Communion	.37*	-.13*	1.00*			
Self Agency	-.13*	.16*	-.41*	1.00*		
Ability to Do Important Tasks	.18*	.07	.01	.06	1.00*	
Ability to Relate	.45*	-.20*	.68*	-.28	-.04	1.00*
Residuals						
Predictor	**Other Communion**	**Other Agency**	**Self Communion**	**Self Agency**	**Ability to Do Important Tasks**	**Ability to Relate**
Other Communion	.87*					
Other Agency	-.28*	.94*				
Self Communion	.30*	-.12*	.94*			
Self Agency	-.04	.14*	-.32*	.88*		
Ability to Do Important Tasks	.19*	.02	.05	.04	.91*	
Ability to Relate	.33*	-.19*	.56*	-.15*	.00	.78*

Note. * indicates $t>1.96$, $p<.05$.

Table 12. Estimated standardized vector autoregression parameters for Model 1 (Symptoms)

Patient A								
	Other Communion (t)	**Other Agency (t)**	**Self Communion (t)**	**Self Agency (t)**	**Self-Esteem (t)**	**Anxiety (t)**	**Depression (t)**	**Stress (t)**
Other Communion (t + 1)	-.01	-	-	-	.05	-.03	-.04	.06
Other Agency (t + 1)	-	.03	-	-	.05	.03	.03	.05
Self Communion (t + 1)	-	-	-.03	-	.03	-.14*	.08	.01
Self Agency (t + 1)	-	-	-	-.02	.02	-.07	-.00	.05
Self-Esteem (t + 1)	-.02	-.03	-.01	.03	.07	-	-	-
Anxiety (t + 1)	.03	-.01	.11*	-.08	-	.26*	-	-
Depression (t + 1)	.06	.07	-.04	-.02	-	-	.06	-
Stress (t + 1)	.05	.13*	.03	.06	-	-	-	.11*
Patient B								
	Other Communion (t)	**Other Agency (t)**	**Self Communion (t)**	**Self Agency (t)**	**Self-Esteem (t)**	**Anxiety (t)**	**Depression (t)**	**Stress (t)**
Other Communion (t + 1)	.40*	.16*	-	-	.10	-.17*	.12	.09
Other Agency (t + 1)	-	.08	-	-	.05	.22*	-.06	-.08
Self Communion (t + 1)	-	-	.32*	-	-.08	-.05	.01	-.14
Self Agency (t + 1)	-.24*	.23*	-	.19*	.07	-.33*	.06	.02
Self-Esteem (t + 1)	.30*	.06	-0.15*	.05	.44*	.15*	-	-
Anxiety (t + 1)	-.30*	.18*	.07	.01	-	-.06	-	-
Depression (t + 1)	-.18*	-.04	.15*	-.05	-	-	.01	-
Stress (t + 1)	-.16*	-.08	.17*	-.04	-	-	-	.26*

Patient C								
	Other Communion (t)	Other Agency (t)	Self Communion (t)	Self Agency (t)	Self-Esteem (t)	Anxiety (t)	Depression (t)	Stress (t)
Other Communion (t + 1)	.00	-.19*	.11	-.10	-.02	-.07	.04	-.06
Other Agency (t + 1)	.17*	.28*	-	-	.09	.03	-.02	.23*
Self Communion (t + 1)	-	-	.19*	-.14*	-.05	-.17*	.12	.06
Self Agency (t + 1)	-	.13*	-	.30*	.29*	.15	-.10	.27*
Self-Esteem (t + 1)	-.12	-.06	.18*	-.06	.12*	-.19*	.19*	-
Anxiety (t + 1)	.16*	.02	-.12	.05	-	.43*	-.21*	-
Depression (t + 1)	.21*	-.20*	.01	.08	-	.26*	.01	-
Stress (t + 1)	.25*	-.01	-.08	.05	-	.35*	-.36*	.26*

Note. * indicates t>1.96, p<.05, - indicates that the parameter was not estimated as part of the model.

Table 13. Estimated standardized vector autoregression parameters for Model 2 (Emotions)

Patient A										
	Other Communion (t)	Other Agency (t)	Self Communion (t)	Self Agency (t)	Happy (t)	Irritable (t)	Sad (t)	Frightened (t)	Angry (t)	Calm (t)
Other Communion (t + 1)	-.02	-	-	-	.04	-.04	-.03	.02	.01	-.01
Other Agency (t + 1)	-	-.01	-	-	.02	.07	-.00	.12*	.00	.05
Self Communion (t + 1)	-	-	-.01	-	-.03	-.03	-.02	-.08	-.00	.02
Self Agency (t + 1)	-	-	-	-.02	.06	-.03	.05	-.04	.06	-.05
Happy (t + 1)	-.06	-.06	.01	-.06	.12*	-	-	-	-	-
Irritable (t + 1)	.04	.16*	-.04	.13*	-	.03	-	-	-	-
Sad (t + 1)	-.01	-.04	-.02	.01	-	-	.07	-	-	-
Frightened (t + 1)	.02	-.01	-.02	.07	-	-	-	.15*	-	-
Angry (t + 1)	.03	.02	.01	.01	-	-	-	-	.07	-
Calm (t + 1)	-.04	-.09*	-.08	-.07	-	-	-	-	-	.20*

Table 13. (Continued)

Patient B										
	Other Communion (t)	**Other Agency (t)**	**Self Communion (t)**	**Self Agency (t)**	**Happy (t)**	**Irritable (t)**	**Sad (t)**	**Frightened (t)**	**Angry (t)**	**Calm (t)**
Other Communion (t + 1)	.46*	-	-	-	-.13*	.08	.01	.05	-.15*	-.04
Other Agency (t + 1)	.24*	.04	-	-	-.21*	.19*	.06	-.09	.10	.11
Self Communion (t + 1)	-	-	.29*	-	-.04	-.02	.00	.10	-.23*	-.08
Self Agency (t + 1)	-.24*	.21*	-	.20*	.06	-.25*	.04	-.02	-.04	-.10
Happy (t + 1)	.26*	-.04	-.10	-.01	.33*	-	-	-	-	-
Irritable (t + 1)	-.07	.14*	.05	.12*	-	.20*	-	-	-	-
Sad (t + 1)	.02	.04	.07	.02	-	-	.30*	-	-	.16*
Frightened (t + 1)	.33*	.01	-.03	-.02	-	.33*	-.30*	.24*	-	-
Angry (t + 1)	.02	.10	.05	.12*	-	-	-	-	.24*	-
Calm (t + 1)	.29*	-.07	-.08	-.10*	-	.19*	-	-	-	.29*
Patient C										
	Other Communion (t)	**Other Agency (t)**	**Self Communion (t)**	**Self Agency (t)**	**Happy (t)**	**Irritable (t)**	**Sad (t)**	**Frightened (t)**	**Angry (t)**	**Calm (t)**
Other Communion (t + 1)	.06	-	-	-	.36*	-.01	.13*	-.17*	.20*	-.11*
Other Agency (t + 1)	-	.15*	-	-	.11	.06	.01	.15*	.10	-.18*
Self Communion (t + 1)	-	-	.16*	-	.14*	.05	-.03	.07	.01	.01
Self Agency (t + 1)	-	-	-	.26*	-.15*	-.03	.16*	-.12	.05	.05
Happy (t + 1)	-.08	-.07	.08	-.01	.28*	-	-	-	-	-
Irritable (t + 1)	-.00	.03	-.01	-.00	-	.16*	-	-	-	-
Sad (t + 1)	-.06	-.16*	.19*	.02	-	-	-.18*	.36*	.23*	-

Patient C										
	Other Communion (t)	**Other Agency (t)**	**Self Communion (t)**	**Self Agency (t)**	**Happy (t)**	**Irritable (t)**	**Sad (t)**	**Frightened (t)**	**Angry (t)**	**Calm (t)**
Frightened (t + 1)	.02	-.15*	-.03	.00	-	-	-.20*	.24*	-	-
Angry (t + 1)	.03	-.06	-.18*	-.01	-	-	-	-	.06	-.12*
Calm (t + 1)	-.06	-.22*	.23*	-.09	-.25*	-	-	-	-	.16*

Note. * indicates t>1.96, p<.05, - indicates that the parameter was not estimated as part of the model.

Table 14. Estimated standardized vector autoregression parameters for Model 3 (Functioning)

Patient A						
	Other Communion (t)	**Other Agency (t)**	**Self Communion (t)**	**Self Agency (t)**	**Ability to Do Important Tasks (t)**	**Ability to Relate (t)**
Other Communion (t + 1)	-.01	-	-	-	-.06	.03
Other Agency (t + 1)	-	.01	-	-	.04	.06
Self Communion (t + 1)	-	-	.01	-	-.04	.00
Self Agency (t + 1)	-	-	-	-.01	-.01	-.01
Ability to Do Important Tasks (t + 1)	.06	.12*	-.02	.10*	.17*	-
Ability to Relate (t + 1)	.00	.01	.03	.01	-	.08
Patient B						
	Other Communion (t)	**Other Agency (t)**	**Self Communion (t)**	**Self Agency (t)**	**Ability to Do Important Tasks (t)**	**Ability to Relate (t)**
Other Communion (t + 1)	.41*	.14*	-	-	-.08	.12
Other Agency (t + 1)	-	.03	-.23*	-	.22*	.06
Self Communion (t + 1)	-	-	.36*	-	-.13*	.09
Self Agency (t + 1)	-	.17*	-	.16*	-.09	.08
Ability to Do Important Tasks (t + 1)	.55*	-.01	-.22*	.10*	.36*	-
Ability to Relate (t + 1)	.33*	.04	-.14*	.03	-	.38*

Table 14. (Continued)

Patient C						
	Other Communion (t)	**Other Agency (t)**	**Self Communion (t)**	**Self Agency (t)**	**Ability to Do Important Tasks (t)**	**Ability to Relate (t)**
Other Communion (t + 1)	.14*	-	-	-	-26*	.16*
Other Agency (t + 1)	-	.20*	-	-	-.05	.06
Self Communion (t + 1)	-	-	.09	-	-.05	.15*
Self Agency (t + 1)	-	-	-	.24*	.08	-.12*
Ability to Do Important Tasks (t + 1)	.31*	.12*	-.25*	-.09	-.05	-
Ability to Relate (t + 1)	-.15*	-.07	.04	-.03	-	.43*

Note. * indicates t>1.96, p<.05, - indicates that the parameter was not estimated as part of the model.

Person Specific Results

Model fit indices for Model 1 (Symptoms), Model 2 (Emotions), and Model 3 (Functioning) for Patients A, B, and C can be found in Table 8. These indices suggested that all three models adequately fit the data for Patient A, all 3 models needed to be modified to adequately fit the data for Patient B, and Models 1 and 2 needed to be modified to adequately fit the data for Patient C. The estimated standardized variance and covariance parameter values at time t and the standardized variance and covariance parameter values for the residuals for each of the models for each patient can be found in Table 9 (Symptoms), Table 10 (Emotions), and Table 11 (Functioning). Finally, the estimated standardized vector autoregression parameters associated with each of the models for each of the patients are presented in Table 12 (Symptoms), Table 13 (Emotions), and Table 14 (Functioning).

Table 15. Summary of Significant Regression Associations for Patient A

Predictors (t)	Associated With (t + 1)
Interpersonal Perception	
Other Agency	Stress (+)
	Irritability (+)
	Ability to Do Important Tasks (+)
	Calm (-)
Self Communion	Anxiety (+)
Self Agency	Irritability (+)
	Ability to Do Important Tasks (+)
Symptoms	
Anxiety	Anxiety (+)
	Communal Behavior (-)
Stress	Stress (+)
Emotions	
Happiness	Happiness (+)
Fear	Agentic Perception (+)
	Fear (+)
Calm	Calm (+)
Functioning	
Ability to Do Important Tasks	Ability to Do Important Tasks (+)

Note. (+) indicates that the regression parameter is positive; (-) indicates that the regression parameter is negative.

Table 16. Summary of Significant Regression Associations for Patient B

Predictors (t)	Associated With (t + 1)
Interpersonal Perception	
Other Communion	Communal Perception (+)
	Self Esteem (+)
	Happiness (+)
	Fear (+)
	Calm (+)
	Ability to Do Important Tasks (+)
	Ability to Relate (+)
	Anxiety (-)
	Depression (-)
	Stress (-)
Other Agency	Anxiety (+)
	Irritability (+)
Self Communion	Communal Behavior (+)
	Depression (+)
	Stress (+)
	Self Esteem (-)
	Ability to Do Important Tasks (-)
	Ability to Relate (-)
Self Agency	Agentic Behavior (+)
	Irritability (+)
	Anger (+)
	Ability to Do Important Tasks (+)
	Calm (-)
Symptoms	
Anxiety	Anxiety (+)
	Communal Behavior (-)
Stress	Stress (+)
Emotions	
Happiness	Happiness (+)
	Communal Perception (-)
	Agentic Perception (-)
Irritable	Agentic Perception (+)
	Irritability (+)
	Fear (+)
	Calm (+)
	Agentic Behavior (-)
Sad	Sadness (+)
	Fear (-)
Fear	Fear (+)

Predictors (t)	Associated With (t + 1)
Anger	Anger (+)
	Communal Perception (-)
	Communal Behavior (-)
Calm	Sadness (+)
	Calm (+)
Functioning	
Ability to Do Important Tasks	Agentic Perception (+)
	Ability to Do Important Tasks (+)
	Communal Behavior (-)
Ability to Relate	Ability to Relate (+)

Note. (+) indicates that the regression parameter is positive; (-) indicates that the regression parameter is negative.

For Patient A (See Table 15 for summary), perceiving agency in others at time t is associated with increased stress, irritability, and ability to do important tasks and decreased calmness at time t + 1. Further, perceiving agency in herself at time t is associated with increased irritability and ability to do important tasks in the next social interaction, while perceiving herself in a communal way at time t is associated with increased anxiety at the following time point. Neither self or other interpersonal perception at time t is associated with the same interpersonal perception at time t + 1. In terms of psychological states, anxiety at time t is associated with viewing herself as less communal at time t + 1, while anger at time t is associated with viewing the other as more agentic at time t + 1. Finally, anxiety, stress, happiness, anger, and calmness at time t are associated with increased anxiety, stress, happiness, anger, and calmness respectively at time t + 1.

For Patient B (See Table 16 for summary), perceiving agency in others at time t is associated with increased anxiety and irritability at time t + 1, while perceiving herself in an agentic way is associated with increased irritability and anger and decreased calm during the next social interaction. In terms of communion, perceiving communion in others at time t is associated with increased self-esteem, happiness, fear, calm, ability to do important tasks and ability to relate and decreased anxiety, depression, and stress during the next social interaction. Perceiving herself more communally at time t is associated with decreased self-esteem, ability to do important tasks, and ability to relate and increased depression and stress at time t + 1. Additionally, perceiving herself as more agentic and communal and perceiving others as more communal at time t are all associated with increases in these same perceptions at time t + 1. In terms of symptoms, self esteem at time t is associated with greater agentic self perception at time t + 1 while greater anxiety at time t predicts less communal other perception, greater agentic other perception, less agentic self perception and greater self esteem at the next time point. In terms of emotions, greater happiness at time t is associated with less communal and agentic other perception at time t + 1, greater irritability at time t is associated with greater agentic other perception, less agentic self perception, greater fear, and greater calm at time t + 1, greater sadness at time t is associated with less fear at time t + 1, greater anger at time t is associated with less communal self and other perception at time t + 1, and greater calm at time t is association with greater sadness at time t + 1. Finally, the ability to do important tasks at time t is associated with greater agentic other perception and less communal self perception at time t + 1. Self-esteem, stress, happiness, irritability, sadness, fear, anger, calm, and ability to relate at time t all predict increases in those psychological states at time t + 1.

For Patient C (see Table 17 for summary), perceiving others as agentic was associated with an increase in ability to do important tasks and decreases in depression, sadness, fear, and calm. In terms of communion, perceiving communion in others at time t was associated with increases in anxiety, depression, stress, and ability to do important tasks, and decreases in her ability to relate during the next social interaction. Perceiving communion in herself at time t is associated with greater self-esteem, sadness, calm, and decreases in anger and ability to do important tasks at the social interaction. Further there is evidence across models that interpersonal perceptions are associated with increases in the same perceptions at time t + 1. In terms of symptoms, self esteem at time t is associated with increased in agentic self perception at time t + 1, anxiety at time t is associated with decreases in communal self perception and self esteem and increases in depression and stress at time t + !, depression at time t is associated with increases in self esteem and decreases in anxiety and stress at time t + 1, and stress at time t is associated with increases in agentic self and other perception at time t + 1. In terms of emotions, happiness at time t is associated with increases in communal self and other perception and decreases in agentic self perception and calm at time t + 1, sadness at time t is associated with increases in communal other perception, increases in agentic self perception, and decreases in anger at time t + 1, fear at time t is associated with decreases in communal other perception and increases in agentic other perception and sadness at time t + 1, anger at time t is associated with increases in communal other perception at time t + 1, and calm at time t is associated with decreases in

Table 17. Summary of Significant Regression Associations for Patient C

Predictors (t)	Associated With (t + 1)
Interpersonal Perception	
Other Communion	Anxiety (+)
	Depression (+)
	Stress (+)
	Ability to Do Important Tasks (+)
	Ability to Relate (-)
Other Agency	Ability to Do Important Tasks (+)
	Depression (-)
	Sadness (-)
	Fear (-)
	Calm (-)
Self Communion	Self Esteem (+)
	Sadness (+)
	Calm (+)
	Anger (-)
	Ability to Do Important Tasks (-)
Self Agency	Agentic Behavior (+)
	Irritability (+)
	Anger (+)
	Calm (-)
Self Esteem	Agentic Behavior (+)
	Self Esteem (+)
Symptoms	
Anxiety	Anxiety (+)
	Depression (+)
	Stress (+)

Table 17. (Continued)

Predictors (t)	**Associated With (t + 1)**
Symptoms	
Anxiety	Communal Behavior (-)
	Self Esteem (-)
Depression	Self Esteem (+)
	Anxiety (-)
	Stress (-)
Stress	Agentic Perception (+)
	Agentic Behavior (+)
	Stress (+)
Emotions	
Happy	Communal Perception (+)
	Communal Behavior (+)
	Happiness (+)
	Agentic Behavior (-)
	Calm (-)
Irritability	Irritability (+)
Sad	Communal Perception (+)
	Agentic Behavior (+)
	Sadness (-)
	Fear (-)
Fear	Agentic Perception (+)
	Sadness (+)
	Fear (+)
	Communal Perception (-)
Anger	Communal Perception (+)
	Sadness (+)
Calm	Calm (+)
	Communal Perception (-)
	Agentic Perception (-)
	Anger (-)
Functioning	
Ability to Do Important Tasks	Ability to Do Important Tasks (+)
Ability to Relate	Communal Perception (+)
	Communal Behavior (+)
	Ability to Relate (+)
	Agentic Behavior (-)

Note. (+) indicates that the regression parameter is positive; (-) indicates that the regression parameter is negative.

communal and agentic other perception and decreases in anger at time t + 1. In terms of functioning, ability to do important tasks at time t is associated with decreased communal other perception at time t + 1 while ability to relate at time t is associated with increased communal self and other perception and decreased agentic self perception at time t + 1. Further, self esteem, anxiety, stress, happiness, irritability, sadness, fear, calm, and ability to relate at time t are associated with increases in the same psychological state at time t + 1.

Discussion

These person specific analyses allow us to describe three different psychotherapy patients through the lens of the interpersonal situation framework and identify possible threats to treatment, internal conflicts, and interpersonal patterns that could be useful to discuss more thoroughly in a therapeutic context. Importantly, in all but one case (Model 3, Patient A and Patient C), the same model could not be applied to multiple patients, and when it could, the significant model parameters differed across patients. This was true regardless of whether the patients had the same diagnosis. This is consistent with other work using person specific approaches and highlights the benefit of this method. For example, Yang et al. (2018) examined 411 person specific networks of associations that included emotions, interpersonal perception, and other variables across people and time periods and none were identical. The following descriptions provide a summary of findings for each patient and highlight important clinical implications.

Patient A (BPD)

For patient A, how she perceives herself and others in one social interaction seems to be unrelated to how she perceives herself and others in the next social interaction. This lack of stability is consistent with the identity diffusion that often characterizes BPD (Jørgensen, 2010) and suggests that interventions that support mentalization, model identity integration, and help the client create a more integrated identity could be useful (e.g., Bateman, Fonagy, & Allen, 2009; Caligor, Kernberg, Clarkin, & Yeomans, 2018). Additionally, perception of agency in others appears to be particularly important for Patient A. After interactions where she perceives others as more agentic, she reports feeling more irritable, more stressed, and less calm, while also reporting an increased ability to do important tasks. This interesting juxtaposition between feeling more negative emotions but also feeling more able to get things done after perceiving agency is something that could continue to be explored further in therapy. If others are dominant, must she subsequently prove herself competent? Or, could this be a sign of potentially effective regulation of negative affect via sublimation into productive activity?

Interestingly and in contrast, perception of communion in others appears unimportant to Patient A. Her symptoms, emotions, and functioning are unrelated to her perception of the other's warmth. This highlights the importance of a person-specific perspective because research by Sadikaj et al. (2013) suggests that there is a relationship at the between person level between perceiving others as cold and negative emotions but we are not seeing that relationship in this specific patient. Further, the patient describes an interesting dynamic when it comes to her own expressions of warmth and friendliness and anxiety. In particular, Patient A reports feeling more anxious after interactions where she perceives herself as warm and friendly. This experience of anxiety then causes the patient to behave in a less friendly, more withdrawn way in future social interactions, perhaps as an attempt to regulate her anxiety. This chaotic cycle of closeness and distance is common in BPD (Russell et al., 2017. This dynamic could have implications for therapy as it impedes alliance formation. Outside of therapy, it might also make it more difficult for the patient to get social support from others in moments where that support could be very helpful to her.

Finally, we see that the client's emotions and symptoms during her first interaction seem to affect her experience of future interactions. Now in some cases (such as when she is feeling happy or calm) this might be useful to the patient, but in other cases (stress, anxiety, fear), this may be detrimental. Patient A seems prone to persistence of negative affect (Kuppens, Allen, & Sheeber, (2010), highlighting the client's emotion regulation deficits, another common characteristic of BPD.

Patient B (BPD)

For Patient B, how she perceives herself and others in one interaction is related to how she perceives herself and others in the next interaction. This suggests greater identity coherence and stability than Patient A, despite the fact that the client received a similar BPD diagnosis. For this patient, anxiety seems to be an important symptom that affects her perceptions of others. After social interactions where she reports feeling anxious, she reports viewing others as less communal and more agentic. This perception of a cold, dominant other is, in turn, associated with a number of problematic outcomes, including lower self esteem, less happiness and calmness, more anxiety, depression, stress, irritability, and decreased functioning. Because of this, helping the client to better regulate her anxiety and understand how her anxiety can influence her psychological experience could help the client avoid this snowball effect, where one psychological symptom leads to an escalating cascade of symptoms in a short period of time.

Additionally, Patient B has an interesting contradiction involving communal perception of self and other. Perceiving others as warm is associated with several positive outcomes including more self-esteem, happiness, calmness, better functioning, and less anxiety, depression, and stress. In contrast, behaving warmly herself is associated with the opposite: lower self-esteem and functioning and more depression and stress. This conflicted pattern may make it difficult for the patient to form close relationships. This pattern can be targeted in therapy by helping the patient become aware of this contradiction and exploring why behaving warmly leaves her feeling so badly (Benjamin, 2003; Cain & Pincus, 2016; Hopwood et al., in press).

Finally, like Patient A, we see that Patient B's symptoms, emotions, and functioning during a social interaction affect her experience of future social interactions. In some cases (such as when she is feeling happy or calm, has high self esteem, or is functioning well) this might be useful. However, the same persistence of negative affect discussed for Patient A is also apparent for Patient B (Kuppens et al. 2010).

Patient C (PTSD)

For Patient C, how she perceives herself and others in one interaction is related to how she perceives herself and others in the next interaction. This suggests a coherent and stable identity, which we might expect given that the client does not have a personality disorder diagnosis. For this patient, perceiving others as warm and dominant and herself as less warm, is associated with an increased ability to do important tasks during future interactions. This pattern suggests that the use of a warm and dominant stance in the course of therapy might even empower the patient with a greater sense of efficacy in her future interactions. Such a pattern also bodes well for the use of cognitive behavioral treatment, which is common for PTSD (Taylor, 2017).

We also see that in some specific cases (happy, ability to relate, and irritability) how she is feeling/functioning during her first interaction seems to affect her experience of future interactions. Given that the patient's irritability is not predicted by her perception of self or other but does seem to carry over from interaction to interaction, it may be helpful to explore and clarify what it is that makes her irritable. In this case, the persistence of irritability may be trauma related and therapy can help her address that irritability when it arises as part of a broader PTSD treatment (Kalkstein, Scott, Vickers Smith, & Cruz, 2018).

Finally, for patient C, we see that happiness and the ability to relate (both positive states) are associated with perceiving self or other as communal. While irritability, unhappiness, and an inability to relate to others (all negative outcomes) are associated with perceiving self or other as agentic. When Patient C is feeling good and capable after an interaction, she tends to perceive others as warm in future interactions but when she is feeling agitated or less capable, she tends to perceive others as dominant in future interactions. This interpersonal pattern where positive psychological states lead to perceptions of communion while negative psychological states lead to perceptions of agency could be useful for the client to be aware of and reflect on over the course of therapy (Benjamin, 2003; Cain & Pincus, 2016).

Precision Assessment

The person specific approach models each patient's data, allowing therapists to identify the individual patient's interpersonal dynamics. This "precision assessment" (Roche & Pincus, 2016) provides the therapist with a richer and more applicable case conceptualization than one drawn from research describing a "prototypical patient" that may or may not exist (e.g., Lewis & Ridenour, in press; Roche et al., 2014). Although this approach highlights variables and dynamics of the interpersonal situation that the clinician may want to pay attention to or explore in the therapeutic setting, it does not explain why the patient exhibits these dynamics. It does, however, provide an initial assessment of the client that can then be expanded upon and even reevaluated over the course of therapy.

General Discussion

Using data from an ECR study of psychotherapy outpatients' social interactions over 21 days, the current analyses extend the existing research on interpersonal dynamics in personality pathology (Benjamin, 1996; Hopwood, 2018b; Pincus, 2005, 2018; Pincus & Hopwood, 2012). In the first approach, multilevel modeling was used to examine severity of personality impairment as a moderator of associations between perceptions of self and psychological state. However, because inferences drawn from multilevel modeling can only be applied to populations as a whole (Molenaar, 2004, 2013; Ram et al., 2017), person specific analyses (Molenaar & Campbell, 2009) were also used to describe the interpersonal dynamics for three individual patients from the sample.

Importantly, findings from the person specific analyses did not simply replicate findings at the population level. At the population level, perceiving others as dominant and controlling is associated with a range of negative outcomes, while perceiving self and others as warm and welcoming is associated with a range of positive outcomes. Examining the dynamics of individual patients, however, suggests that different dynamics may be at play at the person-specific level of analysis. Similar to the multilevel findings, Patient A experiences negative symptoms and emotions following interactions with an agentic other, but does not demonstrate the significant relationships between communal perception of self and other and psychological states found at the population level. Patient B also experiences negative symptoms and emotions following interactions with an agentic other, and experiences increases in self esteem, positive emotions, and functioning following interactions with a communal other. However, she also experiences lower self-esteem and functioning and greater depression and stress following interactions where she perceives herself as warm, a pattern inconsistent with the multilevel analysis. Finally, unlike Patients A and B, Patient C appears to experience less depression, sadness, and fear after interactions with an agentic other. Additionally, contrary to the multilevel findings, Patient C experiences increased symptom expression and a decreased ability to relate after interactions with a warm other and a mix of positive and negative psychological states after perceiving herself as warm. Thus, these analyses demonstrate the benefit of conducting analyses that describe the interpersonal dynamics of the average patient and the danger of applying these findings to specific patients. These analyses also demonstrate the efficacy and utility of a person specific approach, particularly in a clinical context where the goal is to apply inferences to specific patients (Roche & Pincus, 2016).

Despite their differences, both analytic approaches use an ECR design to demonstrate the role of interpersonal perception and behavior on affect, symptoms, and functioning, key aspects of the interpersonal situation and the contemporary interpersonal model of personality pathology. These findings at different levels of analysis add to the existing literature by operationalizing the regulatory and relational processes associated with personality pathology. Previous research has shown that individual differences in psychopathology impact interpersonal perception of self and others (Roche et al., 2013; Russell et al., 2007; Wright et al., 2017) and has examined the relationship between interpersonal perceptions of self and other and symptoms, emotions, and functioning in individuals with different personality disorders and related pathological traits (See Pincus,

2018 for a review). These studies typically focus on specific categorical personality disorder diagnoses (e.g., BPD, NPD) or specific pathological traits (e.g., dependency, narcissism, anxious attachment). The current multilevel analyses extended this work by examining how the general dimension of severity of personality impairment can affect the general associations among elements of the interpersonal situation.

Although approximately two thirds of our sample received a BPD diagnosis at intake, our findings using a dimensional measure of severity of personality impairment differed in important ways from previous work with BPD patients. Prior work investigating BPD has highlighted the influence of communion, particularly low communion, on psychological states (Sadikaj et al., 2010; Sadikaj et al., 2013, Scott et al., 2017). However, our results suggested that when severity of personality impairment was high, perception of passivity and submissiveness in self and other was more strongly related to psychological states than perception of warmth in self and other. Given the emergence of the DSM-5 AMPD and its distinctive partitioning of general personality pathology into level of personality functioning (Criterion A) and individual differences in pathological personality traits (Criterion B), the current research is an important step for better understanding and validating Criterion A and moving the AMPD into mainstream diagnostic assessment. Additionally, studies such as this that examine the interrelationships between interpersonal perception, behavior, symptoms, emotions, and functioning provide further evidence for the validity and utility of the contemporary interpersonal model and the interpersonal situation framework for investigating personality pathology.

Future Directions for Research

The recent emphasis on incorporating temporally dynamic processes and maintenance mechanisms into trait conceptualizations of psychopathology has resulted in the development of the "interpersonal situation" framework (Hopwood, 2018b; Hopwood et al., in press; Pincus,

Hopwood, & Wright, 2015; Pincus et al., in press). Research using this framework specifies inputs, intermediaries, and outputs of clinical interest and importance and provides a systematic lexicon to organize objective and subjective perspectives. Additionally, the development of the contemporary interpersonal model of personality pathology (Pincus, 2005; Pincus & Hopwood, 2012) expands the interpersonal situation framework to describe how it can be used to understand normal and disturbed functioning and identifies the distortion of interpersonal perception as a key component to this distinction. These advances in interpersonal theory have advanced the study of interpersonal dynamics and personality pathology and have set the stage for future research on personality pathology more generally.

Examining Distortion

To successfully navigate the social world, individuals must accurately perceive the important cues they are sending and receiving. Thus, a key component of the contemporary interpersonal model of personality pathology is distortion. Distortions occur when one's interpretation of the interpersonal situation aligns with an alternative, internal, and psychologically impactful or conflictual schema that is often threatening or painful rather than accurately perceiving the other person and the objective characteristics of the situation. Although researchers and clinicians have identified distortion as an important component of the disturbed interpersonal relationships associated with personality pathology, little research has directly examined its dynamic processes and the contexts in which distortion occurs.

One difficulty in assessing distortion is that ECR and other experience sampling approaches are typically limited to an individual's self report and do not typically integrate informant ratings or objective data. Thus, researchers are able to talk about what happens when participants view self and other in a particular way, but often have no way of knowing how distorted that perception might be. Given that distortion seems to theoretically mediate the association between interpersonal perception and behavior, finding ways to directly assess distortion is an important future direction in personality pathology research that could help us understand personality dynamics and highlight possible areas for intervention. For example, wearable sensors such as the Electronic Audio Recorder (Mehl, 2017) could be employed in combination with ECR to compare patients' perceptions of self and other with an audio recording of the same social interaction. Comparing these data would allow for quantification of accuracy or distortion of interpersonal perception. Physiological sensors could also be integrated into ECR designs (Timmons et al., 2017).

Examining Interpersonal Dynamics Across Different Time Scales

Intensive repeated measures and in particular ECR designs have allowed researchers to directly examine personality dynamics using the interpersonal situation framework. However, because the unit of analysis with this approach is typically the interaction as a whole, information about the moment-to-moment dynamics and associated distortions within the interaction is lost in the participant's overall impression of the experience.

Another intensive repeated measures approach that is gaining traction in the study of interpersonal functioning is Continuous Assessment of Interpersonal Dynamics (CAID; Sadler, Ethier, Gunn, Duong, &Woody, 2009), which models the moment-to-moment unfolding of interpersonal behavior in dyadic interactions. In the CAID method, an observer watches a video of a social interaction and uses a computer joystick and joystick monitoring program (Girard & Wright, 2018; Lizdek, Sadler, Woody, Ethier, & Malet, 2012) to continuously (e.g., every half second) record moment-to-moment ratings of one person's social behavior (agency and communion) on a circumplex surface. The position of the joystick relative to the origin captures the target person's momentary interpersonal stance on the IPC and the distance from the origin captures the momentary intensity of that interpersonal stance. Later, the observer re-watches the video, but this time provides a trajectory of the interaction partner's interpersonal behavior over the course of the interaction. The resulting data provide a dense sampling of the reasonably continuous trajectory of the target person's interpersonal behavior over time in terms of agency and communion. Because the continuous trajectories for both interaction partners are exactly coordinated in time, they can be combined to represent and study the various patterns of entrainment that link the interpersonal behavior of the two individuals. Thus, the data produced from the CAID method are inherently dyadic with the interpersonal behavior of each person in the interaction providing an inseparable context for the interpersonal behavior of the other, consistent with the interpersonal situation framework.

The CAID method directly addresses some limitations present in the ECR approach. Specifically, in CAID, the unit of analysis is the interpersonal behavior of each dyad member at each moment of the interaction, allowing for the unfolding dynamics of the interaction to be explicitly examined. Additionally, this approach collects data from both partners of the dyad and tries to limit bias by encouraging a more objective perspective when completing the ratings through the use of video recordings. However, because this approach relies heavily on video recordings rather than naturally occurring social interactions (the one common exception might be a recorded psychotherapy session), the artificial environment of the laboratory and the act of being observed might influence or bias the behavior of the dyads.

Despite this, the CAID approach has allowed researchers to follow and rate the unfolding interaction in the same way that they experience it and to record their moment-to-moment impressions of each person's agentic and communal stance within the context of the larger interaction. Several studies have demonstrated the promising nature of the CAID method for the assessment of interpersonal behavior. Research thus far has demonstrated variability in the degree of entrainment or complementarity at the moment-to-moment level (Sadler et al., 2009), associations between moment-to-moment interpersonal dynamics and task performance (Markey, Lowmaster, & Eichier, 2010), education and clinical applications (Pennings et al., 2014; Sadler, Woody, McDonald, Lizdek, & Little, 2015; Thomas, Hopwood, Woody, Ethier, & Sadler, 2014), the relationship between affect and interpersonal behavior (Ross et al., 2017), and the way psychopathology can influence moment-to-moment interpersonal dynamics (Nilson, Lizdek, & Ethier, 2015; Lizdek, Woody, Sadler, &

Rehman, 2016). Pairing results from finer grained approaches like CAID with research that examines personality dynamics in daily life is an important future direction that capitalizes on the benefits of each approach and compensates for the shortcomings of the other. Both ECR and CAID can effectively operationalize the interpersonal situation framework at different timescales (Pincus et al., in press).

Dimensional Models of Psychopathology

The AMPD is one of a series of efforts to reconceptualize personality and psychopathology as dimensional rather than categorical. These efforts are consistent with research that suggests most constructs in clinical psychology are dimensional in nature and findings that suggest the presence of taxa are likely spurious. In particular, a recent meta-analysis (Haslam et al., 2012) found that only 38.9% research findings suggest the presence of categorical diagnoses and these findings tended to be from older studies that are less methodologically rigorous. After controlling for confounds, these researchers estimated the true prevalence of taxa to be approximately 14%. Thus, there appears to be relatively little evidence of taxa in mood, anxiety, externalizing, and personality disorders. There is, however, substantial evidence for a hierarchy of psychological dimensions. Recently, the HiTOP consortium has been focused on integrating research findings across studies and mental health fields to situate DSM categories in a dimensional hierarchy of psychopathology based on empirical patterns of psychological symptom co-occurrence (Kotov et al., 2017; Krueger et al., 2018). The HITOP model combines psychiatric symptoms and pathological personality trait dimensions to derive a hierarchical model that includes dimensions of internalizing, antagonistic externalizing, impulsive externalizing, thought disorders, somatoform disorders, and detachment at the spectra level of the hierarchy. Below the spectra level, levels range from diagnostic syndromes, to their subfactors, to individual signs and symptoms of psychopathology and maladaptive trait components.

Initial research on the HiTOP dimensions is promising. Twin studies suggest that HiTOP dimensions may better reflect genetic vulnerabilities

and environmental risk factors, neurobiological abnormalities may show clearer and stronger links to HiTOP dimensions, HiTOP dimensions capture illness course more precisely, and these dimensions may better account for functional impairment (see Conway et al., in press for review). Despite this evidence, however, the majority of the studies on personality dynamics focus on one or more categorical diagnostic groups. Thus, the examination of severity of personality impairment as a moderator of dynamic personality and interpersonal processes presented in this chapter represents an important step forward. Future research should continue to examine the moderating role of dimensions, particularly those associated with the AMPD Criterion A and Criterion B, as well as the HiTOP Spectra. Doing so would expand the nomological networks of these transdiagnostic dimensions and capitalize on the meta-framework that interpersonal theory and the interpersonal situation provide. Additionally, although severity of personality impairment significantly moderated the relationship between interpersonal perception and behavior and several psychological outcome variables in the current study, it is possible that a different pathological trait domain or facet associated with the AMPD Criterion B or a HiTOP Spectra might better account for variance in psychological states. Investigating this further could help clinicians better understand why patients with different categorical diagnoses can exhibit similarities in interpersonal dynamics. It might also explain why two patients with the same categorical diagnosis can exhibit different interpersonal dynamics, as was the case in the person-specific models for Patient A and Patient B in this chapter. This information could have important treatment implications moving forward.

CONCLUSION

Methodological and statistical developments have helped to advance personality theory by encouraging the development of a formal testable interpersonal model of personality dynamics that builds upon the principles outlined by interpersonal theory and combines empirically validated

structures with empirically validated dynamic interpersonal processes. In this chapter, we demonstrated how to operationalize the interpersonal situation framework at two levels of analyses to describe important dynamic processes between interpersonal perception of self and other and psychological states. Future research should build upon these advances by examining the role of distortion more explicitly, integrating research using different timescales, and focus on personality dynamics associated with dimensions of personality and psychopathology rather than diagnostic categories.

ACKNOWLEDGMENTS

Author note: This research was supported by grants from the Pennsylvania State University Social Science Research Institute (PI: Levy), and secondary grants to William D. Ellison from a dissertation grant from the Pennsylvania State University Research and Graduate Studies Office, and grants from American Psychoanalytic Association and International Psychoanalytic Association. We thank J. Wesley Scala, M.S., for his assistance in developing training material and coordinating the collection of data, and Kathleen Bohomey, Colin Carey, Caroline Curran, Wendi Falk, Sarah Forsythe, Laura Frey, Caroline Gooch, Jessica Grom, Brittani Hollern, Lauren Lipner, Kristin McLaughlin, Megan Moyer, Joanna Pantelides, Megan Parker, Jacqueline Proczynski, Carolina Ribo, Silvia Rizkallah, Aimee Sohnleitner, and Alyssa Spaw for their assistance in data collection, and Jennifer Fox and Allison Clark for their assistance in the recruitment of participants. We also thank Drs. Peter Molenaar and Joshua Smyth for guidance in the design of the study.

REFERENCES

American Psychiatric Association. (1980). *Diagnostic and statistical manual of mental disorders* (3rd ed.). Arlington, VA: Author.

American Psychiatric Association. (1994). *Diagnostic and statistical manual of mental disorders* (4th ed.). Arlington, VA: Author.

American Psychiatric Association. (2013). *Diagnostic and statistical manual of mental disorders* (5th ed.). Arlington, VA: Auhor.

Bateman, A., Fonagy, P., & Allen, J.G. (2009). *Theory and practice of mentalization based therapy*. Washington, DC: American Psychiatric Publishing.

Bender, D.S., Morey, L.C., & Skodol, A.E. (2011). Toward a model for assessing level of personality functioning in DSM-5, Part I: A review of theory and methods. *Journal of Personality Assessment, 93*, 332-346.

Benjamin, L.S. (1996). *Interpersonal diagnosis and treatment of personality disorders*. New York: Guilford.

Benjamin, L.S. (2003). *Interpersonal reconstructive therapy*. New York: Guilford.

Bryk, A.S., & Raudenbush, S.W. (1992) *Hierarchical linear models: Applications and data analysis methods.* Thousand Oaks, CA, US: Sage Publications, Inc.

Cain, N.M., & Pincus, A.L. (2016). Treating maladaptive interpersonal signatures. In Livesley, W.J., Dimaggio, G.S., & Clarkin, J.F. (Eds.), *Integrated treatment for personality disorder: A modular approach* (pp. 305-324). New York, NY: Guilford Press.

Caligor, E., Kernberg, O.F., Clarkin, J.F., & Yeomans, F.E. (2018). *Psychodynamic therapy for personality disorders: Treating self and interpersonal dysfunction*. Washington, DC: American Psychiatric Press.

Clark, L.A., Livesley, W.J., & Morey, L.C. (1997). Personality disorder assessment: The challenge of construct validity. *Journal of Personality Disorders, 11,* 205-231.

Conway, C.C., Forbes, M.K., Forbush, K.T., Fried, E.I., Hallquist, M.N., Kotov, R.,… & Eaton, N.R. (in press). A hierarchical taxonomy of psychopathology can transform mental health research. *Perspectives on Psychological Science*.

Dawood, S., Dowgwillo, E.A., Wu, L.Z., & Pincus, A.L. (2018). Contemporary Integrative Interpersonal Theory of Personality. In V. Zeigler-Hill and T. Shackleford (Eds.), *The SAGE handbook of personality and individual differences—Vol. 1: The science of personality and individual differences* (pp. 171-202). Los Angeles, CA: Sage.

Decker, H.S. (2013). *The making of DSM-III: A diagnostic manual's conquest of American psychiatry*. New York: Oxford University Press.

Dowgwillo, E.A., Roche, M.J., & Pincus, A.L. (in press). Examining the interpersonal nature of Criterion A of the DSM-5 Section III Alternative Model for Personality Disorders using bootstrapped confidence intervals for the interpersonal circumplex. *Journal of Personality Assessment.*

Eaton, N.R., South, S.C., & Krueger, R.F. (2009). The Cognitive-Affective Processing System (CAPS) approach to personality and the concept of personality disorder: Integrating clinical and social-cognitive research. *Journal of Research in Personality*, *43*, 208-217.

Freud, S. (1914). On narcissism. In J. Strachey (Ed. and Trans.), *The standard edition of the complete psychological works of Sigmund Freud* (Vol. XIV, pp. 66-102). London, England: Hogarth Press.

Girard, J., & Wright, A.G.C. (2018). DARMA: Software for dual axis rating and media annotation. *Behavior Research Methods, 50*, 902-909.

Haslam, N., Holland, E., & Kuppens, P. (2012). Categories versus dimensions in personality and psychopathology: A quantitative review of taxometric research. *Psychological Medicine*, *42*, 903-920.

Hoffman, D.A., & Gavin, M.B. 1998. Centering decisions in hierarchical linear models: Implications for research in organizations. *Journal of Management.* 24, 623-641.

Hopwood, C.J. (2018a). A framework for treating DSM- 5 Alternative Model for Personality Disorder features. *Personality and Mental Health*, *12*, 107-125.

Hopwood, C.J. (2018b). Interpersonal dynamics in personality and personality disorders. *European Journal of Personality, 32,* 499-524.

Hopwood, C.J., Pincus, A.L., & Wright, A.G.C. (in press). The interpersonal situation: Integrating personality assessment, case formulation, and intervention. In D.B. Samuel & D.R. Lynam (Eds.), *Using basic personality research to inform personality disorders*. New York: Oxford University Press.

Hopwood, C.J., Wright, A.G.C., Ansell, E.B., & Pincus, A.L. (2013). The interpersonal core of personality pathology. *Journal of Personality Disorders, 27*, 270-295.

Hopwood, C.J., Zimmermann, J., Pincus, A.L., & Krueger, R.F. (2015). Connecting personality structure and dynamics: Towards a more evidence based and clinically useful diagnostic scheme. *Journal of Personality Disorders, 29*, 431-448.

Huprich, S.K., & Nelson, S.M. (2015). Advancing the assessment of personality pathology with the cognitive-affective processing system. *Journal of Personality Assessment*, *97*, 467-477.

Jöreskog, K.G., & Sörbom, D. (2012). *LISREL (Version 9.10).* Chicago, IL: Scientific Software International.

Jørgensen, C.R. (2010). Invited essay: Identity and borderline personality disorder. *Journal of Personality Disorders, 24,* 344-364.

Kalkstein, S., Scott, J.C., Vickers Smith, R., & Cruz, J. (2018). Effectiveness of an anger control program among veterans with PTSD and other mental health issues: A comparative study. *Journal of Clinical Psychology, 74,* 1422-1430.

Kotov, R., Krueger, R.F., Watson, D. Achenbach, T.M., Althoff, R.R., Bagby, R.M., … & Zimmerman, M. (2017). The Hierarchical Taxonomy of Psychopathology (HiTOP): A dimensional alternative to traditional nosologies. *Journal of Abnormal Psychology, 126,* 454-477.

Krueger, R.F. (2013). Personality disorders are the vanguard of the post-DSM-5.0 era. *Personality Disorders: Theory, Research, and Treatment, 4*, 355-362.

Krueger, R.F., Kotov, R., Watson, D., Forbes, M.K., Eaton, N.R., Ruggero, C.J.,… & Zimmerman, J. (2018). Progress in achieving quantitative classification of psychopathology. *World Psychiatry, 17,* 282-293.

Krueger, R.F., & Markon, K.E. (2014). The role of the DSM-5 personality trait model in moving toward a quantitative and empirically based approach to classifying personality and psychopathology. *Annual Review of Clinical Psychology, 10*, 477-501.

Krueger, R.F., Skodol, A.E., Livesley, W.J., Shrout, P.E., & Huang, Y. (2007). Synthesizing dimensional and categorical approaches to personality disorders: Refining the research agenda for DSM- V Axis II. *International Journal of Methods in Psychiatric Research, 16*, 65-73.

Kupfer, D.J., First, M.B., & Regier, D.A. (2002). *A Research Agenda for DSM-V*. Arlington, VA: American Psychiatric Association.

Kuppens, P., Allen, N.B., & Sheeber, L.B. (2010). Emotional inertia and psychological maladjustment. *Psychological Science, 21*, 984-991.

Lewis, K., & Ridenour, J. (in press). The integration of EMA and single-occasion multimethod assessment data for a complex psychiatric patient. *Assessment*.

Lizdek, Ivana, Pamela Sadler, Erik Woody, Nicole Ethier, and Giles Malet. "Capturing the stream of behavior: A computer-joystick method for coding interpersonal behavior continuously over time." *Social Science Computer Review* 30, no. 4 (2012): 513-521.

Lizdek, Ivana, Erik Woody, Pamela Sadler, and Uzma S. Rehman. "How do depressive symptoms in husbands and wives relate to the interpersonal dynamics of marital interactions?." *Journal of counseling psychology* 63, no. 6 (2016): 721.

Markey, Patrick, Sara Lowmaster, and Wendy Eichler. "A real- time assessment of interpersonal complementarity." *Personal Relationships* 17, no. 1 (2010): 13-25.

Matlab, U.S.G. (1760). *Matlab*. The Mathworks Inc., Natick, MA, *2015*.

Mehl, M.R. (2017). The electronically activated recorder (EAR): A method for the naturalistic observation of daily social behavior. *Current Directions in Psychological Science, 26,* 184-190.

Molenaar, P.C.M. (2004). A manifesto on psychology as idiographic science: Bringing the person back into scientific psychology, this time forever. *Measurement, 2*, 201-218.

Molenaar, P.C.M. (2013). On the necessity to use person-specific data analysis approaches in psychology. *European Journal of Developmental Psychology*, *10*, 29-39.

Molenaar, P.C.M., & Campbell, C.G. (2009). The new person-specific paradigm in psychology. *Current directions in psychological science*, *18*, 112-117.

Morey, L.C., Berghuis, H., Bender, D.S., Verheul, R., Krueger, R.F., & Skodol, A.E. (2011). Toward a model for assessing level of personality functioning in DSM–5, Part II: Empirical articulation of a core dimension of personality pathology. *Journal of Personality Assessment*, *93*, 347-353.

Moskowitz, D.S. (2009). Coming full circle: Conceptualizing the study of interpersonal behaviour. *Canadian Psychology/Psychologie canadienne, 50*, 33-41.

Moskowitz, D.S., & Sadikaj, G. (2012). Event-contingent recording. In M.R. Mehl & T.S. Conner (Eds.), *Handbook of research methods for studying daily life* (pp. 160-175). New York, NY, US: Guilford Press.

Pennings, Helena J.M., Jan van Tartwijk, Theo Wubbels, Luce CA Claessens, Anna C. van der Want, and Mieke Brekelmans. "Real-time teacher–student interactions: A dynamic systems approach." *Teaching and Teacher Education* 37 (2014): 183-193.

Pincus, A.L. (2005). A contemporary integrative interpersonal theory of personality disorders. In M.F. Lenzenweger & J.F. Clarkin (Eds.), *Major theories of personality disorder* (2nd Ed.) (pp. 282-331). New York: Guilford.

Pincus, A.L. (2011). Some comments on nomology, diagnostic process, and narcissistic personality disorder in the DSM-5 proposal for personality and personality disorders. *Personality Disorders: Theory, Research, and Treatment, 2*, 41-53.

Pincus, A.L. (2013). In through the outdoor: Commentary on "Personality Disorders are The Vanguard of the post-DSM-5.0 Era." *Personality Disorders: Theory, Research, and Treatment, 4*, 363-364.

Pincus, A.L. (2018). An interpersonal perspective on Criteria A of the DSM-5 Alternative Model for Personality Disorders. *Contemporary Opinion in Psychology, 21*, 11-17.

Pincus, A.L., & Ansell, E.B. (2013). Interpersonal theory of personality. In J. Suls & H. Tennen (Eds.), *Handbook of psychology—Vol. 5: Personality and social psychology* (2nd Ed., pp. 141-159). Hoboken, NJ: Wiley.

Pincus, A.L., & Hopwood, C.J. (2012). A contemporary interpersonal model of personality pathology and personality disorder. In T.A. Widiger (Ed.), *Oxford Handbook of Personality Disorders* (pp. 372-398). New York, NY: Oxford University Press.

Pincus, A.L., Hopwood, C.J., & Wright, A.G.C. (2015). The situation through an interpersonal lens. *European Journal of Personality, 29*, 407-408.

Pincus, A.L., Hopwood, C.J., & Wright, A.G.C. (in press). The interpersonal situation: An integrative framework for the study of personality, psychopathology, and psychotherapy. In D. Funder, J.F. Rauthmann, & R. Sherman (Eds.), *Oxford handbook of psychological situations*. New York: Oxford University Press.

Pincus, A.L., & Roche, M.J. (in press). Paradigms of personality assessment and level of personality functioning (Criterion A) in the DSM-5 Alternative Model for Personality Disorders. In Hopwood, C.J. & Waugh, M. (Eds.), *The DSM-5 Alternative Model for Personality Disorders: Integrating multiple paradigms of personality assessment*. Oxon, UK: Taylor & Francis Publishers.

Pincus, A.L., Sadler, P., Woody, E., Roche, M.J., Thomas, K.M., & Wright, A.G.C. (2014). Multimethod assessment of interpersonal dynamics. In C.J. Hopwood & R.F. Bornstein (Eds.), *Multimethod clinical assessment* (pp. 51-91). New York: Guilford.

Pincus, A.L., & Wright, A.G.C. (2011). Interpersonal diagnosis of psychopathology. In L.M. Horowitz & S. Strack (Eds.), *Handbook of interpersonal psychology: Theory, research, assessment, and therapeutic interventions* (pp. 359-381), Hoboken, NJ: Wiley.

Pincus, A.L., & Wright, A.G.C. (in press). Narcissism as the dynamics of grandiosity and vulnerability. In S. Doering, H-P. Hartmann, & O.F. Kernberg (Eds.), *Narzissmus: Grundlagen - Störungsbilder - Therapie* (2nd ed.). Stuttgart, Germany: Schattauer Publishers.

Nilsen, Elizabeth S., Ivana Lizdek, and Nicole Ethier. "Mother-child interpersonal dynamics: The influence of maternal and child ADHD symptoms." *Journal of Experimental Psychopathology* 6, no. 4 (2015): jep-047015.

Ram, N., Brinberg, M., Pincus, A.L., & Conroy, D.E. (2017). The questionable ecological validity of ecological momentary assessment: Considerations for design and analysis. *Research in Human Development, 14*, 253-270.

Reich, W. (1949). *Character-analysis* (3rd Ed.) Oxford: Orgone Institute Press.

Roche, M.J., & Pincus, A.L. (2016). Precision assessment: An individualized and temporally dynamic approach to understanding patients in their daily lives. In U. Kumar (Ed.), *The Wiley Handbook of Personality Assessment* (pp.192-204), Hoboken, NJ: Wiley Blackwell.

Roche, M.J., Pincus, A.L., Conroy, D.E., Hyde, A.L., & Ram, N. (2013). Pathological narcissism and interpersonal behavior in daily life. *Personality Disorders: Theory, Research, and Treatment, 4,* 315-323.

Roche, M.J., Pincus, A.L., Hyde, A.L., Conroy, D.E., & Ram, N. (2013). Within-person co-variation of agentic and communal perceptions: Implications for interpersonal theory and assessment. *Journal of Research in Personality, 47*, 445-552.

Roche, M.J., Pincus, A.L., Rebar, A.L., Conroy, D.E., & Ram, N. (2014). Enriching psychological assessment using a person-specific analysis of interpersonal processes in daily life. *Assessment, 21*, 515-528.

Ross, Jaclyn M., Jeffrey M. Girard, Aidan G.C. Wright, Joseph E. Beeney, Lori N. Scott, Michael N. Hallquist, Sophie A. Lazarus, Stephanie D. Stepp, and Paul A. Pilkonis. "Momentary patterns of covariation between specific affects and interpersonal behavior: Linking relationship science and personality assessment." *Psychological assessment* 29, no. 2 (2017): 123.

Russell, J.J., Moskowitz, D.S., Zuroff, D.C., Sookman, D., & Paris, J. (2007). Stability and variability of affective experience and interpersonal behavior in borderline personality disorder. *Journal of Abnormal Psychology, 116*, 578-588.

Sadikaj, G., Moskowitz, D.S., Russell, J.J., Zuroff, D.C., & Paris, J. (2013). Quarrelsome behavior in borderline personality disorder: Influence of behavioral and affective reactivity to perceptions of others. *Journal of Abnormal Psychology, 122*, 195-207.

Sadikaj, G., Moskowitz, D.S., & Zuroff, D.C. (2011). Attachment-related affective dynamics: Differential reactivity to others' interpersonal behavior. *Journal of Personality and Social Psychology, 100*, 905-917.

Sadikaj, G., Russell, J.J., Moskowitz, D.S., & Paris, J. (2010). Affect dysregulation in individuals with borderline personality disorder: Persistence and interpersonal triggers. *Journal of Personality Assessment, 92*, 490-500.

Sadler, P., Ethier, N., Gunn, G.R., Duong, D., & Woody, E. (2009). Are we on the same wavelength? Interpersonal complementarity as shared cyclical patterns during interactions. *Journal of personality and social psychology*, *97*(6), 1005.

Sadler, P., Woody, E., McDonald, K., Lizdek, I., & Little, J. (2015). A lot can happen in a few minutes: Examining dynamic patterns within an interaction to illuminate the interpersonal nature of personality disorders. *Journal of personality disorders*, *29*(4), 526-546.

Schneider, K. (1950). *The psychopathic personalities* (9th Ed.). Vienna: Franz Deuticke.

Scott, L.N., Wright, A.G.C., Beeney, J.E., Lazarus, S.A., Pilkonis, P.A., & Stepp, S.D. (2017). Borderline personality disorder symptoms and aggression: A within-person process model. *Journal of Abnormal Psychology, 126*, 429-440.

Sharp, C., Wright, A.G.C., Fowler, J.C., Frueh, B.C., Allen, J.G., Oldham, J., & Clark, L.A. (2015). The structure of personality pathology: Both general ('g') and specific ('s') factors? *Journal of Abnormal Psychology, 124,* 387-398.

Skodol, A.E. (2012). Personality disorders in DSM-5. *Annual Review of Clinical Psychology, 8*, 317-344.

Taylor, S. (2017). *Clinician's guide to PTSD: A cognitive-behavioral approach.* New York: Guilford.

Thomas, Katherine M., Christopher J. Hopwood, Erik Woody, Nicole Ethier, and Pamela Sadler. "Momentary assessment of interpersonal process in psychotherapy." *Journal of counseling psychology* 61, no. 1 (2014): 1.

Timmons, A.C., Baucom, B.R., Han, S.C., Perrone, L., Chaspari, T., Narayanan, S.S., & Margolin, G. (2017). New frontiers in ambulatory assessment: Big data methods for capturing couples' emotions, vocalizations, and physiology in daily life. *Social Psychological and Personality Science, 8,* 552-563.

Tuarob, S., Tucker, C.S., Kumara, S., Giles, C.L., Pincus, A.L., Conroy, D.E., & Ram, N. (2017). How are you feeling?: A personalized methodology for predicting mental states from temporally observable physical and behavioral information. *Journal of Biomedical Informatics, 68,* 1-19.

Verheul, R., & Widiger, T.A. (2004). A meta-analysis of the prevalence and usage of the personality disorder not otherwise specified (PDNOS) diagnosis. *Journal of Personality Disorders, 18,* 309-319.

Wang, S., Roche. M.J., Pincus, A.L., Conroy, D.E., Rebar, A.L., & Ram, N. (2014). Interpersonal dependency and emotion in everyday life. *Journal of Research in Personality, 53,* 5-12.

Waugh, M., Hopwood, C.J., Krueger, R.F., Morey, L.C., Pincus, A.L., & Wright, A.G.C. (2017). Psychological assessment with the DSM-5 Alternative Model for Personality Disorders: Tradition and innovation. *Professional Psychology: Research and Practice, 48,* 79-89.

Widiger, T.A., & Samuel, D.B. (2005). Diagnostic categories or dimensions? A question for the Diagnostic and Statistical Manual of Mental Disorders--Fifth edition. *Journal of Abnormal Psychology, 114,* 494-505.

Widiger, T.A., & Simonsen, E. (2005). Alternative dimensional models of personality disorder: Finding a common ground. *Journal of Personality Disorders, 19*, 110-130.

Widiger, T.A., & Trull, T.J. (2007). Plate tectonics in the classification of personality disorder: Shifting to a dimensional model. *American Psychologist*, *62*, 71-83.

Wiggins, J.S. (1991). Agency and communion as conceptual coordinates for the understanding and measurement of interpersonal behavior. In D. Cicchetti & W.M. Grove (Eds.), *Thinking clearly about psychology: Essays in honor of Paul E. Meehl, Vol. 2: Personality and psychopathology* (pp. 89-113). Minneapolis, MN: University of Minnesota Press.

Wiggins, J.S. (1996). An informal history of the interpersonal circumplex tradition. *Journal of Personality Assessment, 66,* 217-233.

Wright, A.G.C. (2014). Integrating trait- and process-based conceptualizations of pathological narcissism in the DSM-5 era. In A. Besser (Ed.), *Handbook of the psychology of narcissism: Diverse perspectives* (pp. 153-173). Hauppauge, NY, US: Nova Science Publishers.

Wright, A.G., Hallquist, M.N., Stepp, S.D., Scott, L.N., Beeney, J.E., Lazarus, S.A., & Pilkonis, P.A. (2016). Modeling heterogeneity in momentary interpersonal and affective dynamic processes in borderline personality disorder. *Assessment*, *23*, 484-495.

Wright, A.G.C., Pincus, A.L., Hopwood, C.J., Thomas, K.M., Markon, K.E., & Krueger, R.F. (2012). An interpersonal analysis of pathological personality traits in DSM-5. *Assessment, 19*, 263-275.

Wright, A.G.C., Stepp, S.D., Scott, L.N., Hallquist, M.N., Beeney, J.E., Lazarus, S.A., & Pilkonis, P.A. (2017). The effect of pathological narcissism on interpersonal and affective processes in social interactions. *Journal of Abnormal Psychology, 126*, 898-910.

Yang, X., Ram, N., Gest, S.D., Lydon-Staley, D.M., Conroy, D.E., Pincus, A.L., & Molenaar, P.M.C. (2018). Socioemotional dynamics of emotion regulation and depressive symptoms: A person-specific network approach. *Complexity, 2018*, Article ID 5094179. 14 pages, 2018. https://10.1155/2018/5094179.

Zachar, P., Krueger, R.F., & Kendler, K.S. (2016). Personality disorder in DSM-5: An oral history. *Psychological Medicine*, *46*, 1-10.

In: Personality Disorders
Editors: Levi I. Truslow et al.
ISBN: 978-1-53615-139-8
© 2019 Nova Science Publishers, Inc.

Chapter 3

VALIDITY OF A BRIEF MEASURE OF DSM-5 MALADAPTIVE PERSONALITY TRAITS IN A BLACK COLLEGE SAMPLE

Matthew M. Yalch[1,*], Hans S. Schroder[2] and Sindes Dawood[3]
[1]Palo Alto University, Palo Alto, CA, US
[2]McLean Hospital, Belmont, MA, US
[3]The Pennsylvania State University, State College, PA, US

ABSTRACT

There has been increased interest in conceptualizing and assessing personality disorders in terms of maladaptive personality traits. Recent research in this domain has focused on a specific instrument for measuring maladaptive trails, the *Personality Inventory for DSM-5* (PID-5), which was developed for the formal trait model listed in Section III of DSM-5. Although a growing number of studies have suggested the structural and criterion validity of the traits measured by the PID-5, these

* Corresponding Author Email: myalch@paloaltou.edu.

studies used almost exclusively White samples. Research has been perhaps most notably absent on individuals identifying as Black/African American, who constitute the largest racial minority group in the U.S. In this study we examine the structural and criterion validity of a brief form of the PID-5 in a sample of college students identifying as Black/African American. Consistent with previous research, results suggest that the measure conforms to a higher-order five-factor structure. However, results also indicate that traits are associated with depressive symptoms and alcohol use in different ways than in White samples, suggesting differences in the criterion validity of maladaptive traits across race. These findings have ramifications for the assessment of maladaptive traits cross-culturally and point toward directions for future research.

INTRODUCTION

Maladaptive personality traits and the methods used to assess these traits have been a focus of clinically oriented research in recent years. This research has been informative in clinical assessment and practice (Hopwood, Zimmermann, Pincus, & Krueger, 2015; Rodriguez-Seijas, Eaton, & Krueger, 2015). However, this work has largely been based on samples of White college students, and the validity of maladaptive trait models and assessment methods has been limited with respect to students of other racial backgrounds. One sub-population of particular interest in the U.S. includes individuals identifying as Black or African-American. Black Americans are the country's largest racial minority group, constituting approximately 13% of the total U.S. population (U.S. Census Bureau, 2015) and approximately 14% of post-secondary education enrollment (behind self-identified White [58%] and Latinx [16%], students; National Center of Education Statistics, 2015). Given the prominence of people identifying as Black in the U.S. in general and in post-secondary education in particular, examining the validity of maladaptive personality trait measures for Black college students is of interest to cross-cultural researchers.

MALADAPTIVE PERSONALITY TRAITS

Maladaptive personality traits are increasingly used in the assessment, conceptualization, and diagnosis of psychopathology (Hopwood & Sellbom, 2013; Krueger & Markon, 2014; Rodriguez-Seijas et al., 2015). Proponents of assessing maladaptive traits argue that using maladaptive traits clinically allows for more nuanced, individualized, and evidence-based diagnoses of personality disorders (PDs) and related problems, and provides a bridge to research on basic personality science (Krueger & Markon, 2014; South, Krueger, & Oltmanns, 2011; Widiger et al., 2012). These ideas are reflected in Section III of the current edition of the *Diagnostic and Statistical Manual of Mental Disorders* (DSM-5; American Psychiatric Association [APA], 2013), which includes an alternative model of diagnosing personality problems in terms of five maladaptive trait domains (Antagonism, Detachment, Disinhibition, Negative Affect, and Psychoticism) and facets of these domains. These traits resemble maladaptive extremes of the Five-Factor Model (FFM) traits, which are widely used in normative (i.e., non-maladaptive) personality trait research and which have been broadly replicated cross-culturally (Costa & McCrae, 1992; McCrae & Costa, 2008).

Recent research on the maladaptive traits adopted in DSM-5 has been concentrated on a measure of maladaptive traits that was developed alongside the formal diagnostic model, the *Personality Inventory for DSM-5* (PID-5; Krueger, Derringer, Markon, Watson, & Skodol, 2012). A number of studies on the PID-5 has suggested that the maladaptive traits of the DSM-5 trait model adhere to a factor structure that aligns with that of normative FFM traits (e.g., Gore & Widiger, 2013; Thomas et al., 2013) as well with other models of maladaptive traits organized around a maladaptive FFM (e.g., Anderson et al., 2013; Wright & Simms, 2014). Research has also demonstrated the criterion validity of the PID-5 traits. Specifically, studies indicate that Detachment and Negative Affect are associated with internalizing problems (e.g., symptoms of depression), and that Disinhibition is associated with externalizing problems (e.g., disordered use of alcohol and other substances) (e.g., Creswell, Bachrach, Wright, Pinto, & Ansell, 2016; Few et al., 2013; Zimmerman et al., 2014). The research on the PID-5 and the DSM-5 maladaptive traits more generally has suggested a model of trait assessment that is structurally and criterion valid, and that can be measured reliably (Al-Dajani, Gralnick, & Bagby, 2016).

Cross-Cultural Generalizability of DSM-5/PID-5 Traits

One assumption is that owing in part to their link to normative FFM traits, analogues of which can be found cross-culturally, research on the DSM-5 maladaptive traits (specifically as operationalized using the PID-5) can be generalized to different cultures. However, the PID-5 (as well as other measures of DSM-5 traits; e.g., Simms et al., 2011) was developed and studied in predominantly White samples drawn primarily from the U.S. and to a lesser extent from Europe (for psychometric review, see Al-Dajani et al., 2016). While there has been recent research examining the structural invariance of DSM-5 traits across sex (e.g., Suzuki et al., 2018), studies on the DSM-5 traits with respect to other demographic factors has been limited. This paucity of cross-cultural research has led to calls for more studies on the validation of maladaptive trait assessment measures in other cultures, given that the validity (structural, criterion-related, etc.) of traits and trait assessment methods may differ depending on race, ethnicity, culture, etc. (Allik, 2006; Mulder, 2012).

The necessity for increased research on the validity of maladaptive traits is especially salient for people identifying as Black. In addition to constituting the largest racial minority group in the U.S., Black Americans have had a unique history of oppressive and exploitative treatment at the hands of the majority White population (Kelly, 2006; Neville & Pieterse, 2009; West, 1994). The experience of and adaptation to conditions of this history have been linked to racial differences in personality style and trait composition (e.g., cultural alienation; Grier & Cobbs, 1968; Kambon, 2003; c.f., Kambon & Bowen-Reid, 2009). These differences may be especially apparent in samples of Black college students, who are not only often separated from familiar community support networks, but who are also often exposed to additional race-based stress by virtue of their immersion with White and other non-Black students (e.g., Blume et al., 2011; Harwood et al., 2012; Nadal et al., 2014; Rankin & Reason, 2005). Indeed, research suggests that Black Americans may differ from White Americans in terms of maladaptive trait characteristics (e.g., see McGilloway, Hall, Lee, & Bhui, 2010). However, Black Americans, college student and otherwise, have been traditionally underrepresented in psychology research in general and in personality trait research in particular (Guthrie, 1998). Because of this, the validity of maladaptive trait assessment in Black samples remains largely unexamined.

CURRENT STUDY

In this study we examined the structural and criterion validity of a maladaptive personality trait assessment measure in a sample of Black college students. We based our hypotheses on previous research on predominantly White samples, albeit with the expectation that our results may differ from previous findings given potential personality-related differences across samples with different racial, ethnic, and cultural identities. Specifically, we hypothesized that our assessment of maladaptive traits would conform to the factor structure of the FFM. We also hypothesized that maladaptive traits would demonstrate criterion validity similar to that demonstrated in previous studies. Namely, we expected that (1) Detachment and Negative Affect would be associated with internalizing problems (as indicated by depressive symptoms), and (2) Disinhibition would be associated with externalizing problems (as indicated by excessive alcohol use).

METHOD

Participants

Participants were 124 self-identified Black students enrolled at a large public university in the Midwestern U.S. who participated in a larger study of college student mental health (N = 1026; Schroder et al., 2016, 2017). Participants had a mean age of 20 years (SD = 2 years) and the majority (78%) were female. The breakdown in terms of college class was 38% freshman, 21% sophomore, 21% junior, and 20% senior. Participants responded to online questionnaires after completing a consent form and received course credit for their participation in the study. The procedures of this study were approved by the local Institutional Review Board.

Measures

We assessed constructs of interest using a battery of well-validated assessment measures. Inter-item consistency for each scale (i.e., Cronbach's alpha) is listed in Table 2. Each scale composite was calculated using the average of item responses and then standardized across the whole sample before use in subsequent analyses.

Maladaptive Personality Traits

We assessed maladaptive traits using the brief form of the *Personality Inventory for DSM-5* (PID-5-BF; Krueger et al., 2012). The PID-5-BF is a 25-item questionnaire measuring the five broad maladaptive personality trait domains (Antagonism, Detachment, Disinhibition, Negative Affect, and Psychoticism) listed in Section III of DSM-5 (APA, 2013). Examples of items include "I get emotional easily, often for very little reason" (Negative Affect) and "I feel like I act totally on impulse" (Disinhibition). Participants rated items on a 4-point scale ranging from "very false or often false" to "very true or often true."

Internalizing and Externalizing Problems

We assessed internalizing problems using the Anhedonic Depression subscale of the *Mood and Anxiety Symptom Questionnaire* (MASQ-AD; Watson & Clark, 1991), a 21-item questionnaire measuring anhedonic symptoms of depression (example item: "felt like nothing was very enjoyable"). Participants rated items on a 5-point scale ranging from "not at all" to "extremely." We assessed externalizing problems using the alcohol use short form of the *Patient-Reported Outcome Measurement Information System* (PROMIS-Alc; Pilkonis et al., 2013), a 7-item questionnaire measuring excessive alcohol use in the past 30 days (example item: "I spent too much time drinking"). Participants rated items on a 5-point scale ranging from "never" to "almost always."

Data Analysis

We examined structural validity using exploratory factor analysis (EFA; for reviews of the use of EFA in PD/maladaptive trait research see South & Jarnecke, 2017; Wright, 2017), entering each item from the PID-5-BF as a variable in the analysis. We determined the number of factors using parallel analysis (Horn, 1965), estimated the EFA model using a maximum likelihood estimation, and rotated factors using oblique Promax rotation. Of note given previous research indicating substantial cross-loadings of items on maladaptive trait factor domains (e.g., Wright & Simms, 2014), Promax rotation deals with interstitial loadings between factors efficiently.

We examined criterion validity using bivariate correlations between all variables and multiple linear regression in which we regressed internalizing and externalizing problems onto the five maladaptive trait domains. Consistent with recent trends in research methodology (e.g., Cumming, 2012, 2014), we focused our interpretation of criterion validity analyses on effect size and quantified our regression coefficients using confidence intervals (CIs).

RESULTS

Table 1. EFA factor loadings

1. People would describe me as reckless.	**.68**	-.18	.15	-.12	.16
2. I feel like I act totally on impulse.	**.82**	-.12	-.04	-.07	.19
3. Even though I know better, I can't stop making rash decisions.	**.66**	.07	-.13	.13	.11
4. I often feel like nothing I do really matters.	.02	**.36**	.25	**.31**	.06
5. Others see me as irresponsible.	**.57**	.07	.38	-.01	-.24
6. I'm not good at planning ahead.	**.36**	.12	-.04	**.32**	-.08
7. My thoughts often don't make sense to others.	**.47**	-.05	-.15	.02	**.50**
8. I worry about almost everything.	-.12	**.62**	-.04	.12	.22
9. I get emotional easily, often for very little reason.	-.04	**.62**	-.22	.00	.14
10. I fear being alone in life more than anything else.	-.17	**.70**	.22	-.13	.13
11. I get stuck on one way of doing things, even when it's clear it won't work.	.22	**.68**	.03	.05	-.29
12. I have seen things that weren't really there.	**.38**	**.33**	-.08	-.11	.23
13. I steer clear of romantic relationships.	.19	.14	.14	**.36**	-.15
14. I'm not interested in making friends.	-.06	-.07	-.18	**.92**	-.04
15. I get irritated easily by all sorts of things.	-.01	.23	-.02	**.30**	**.31**
16. I don't like to get too close to people.	-.11	.00	.01	**.58**	.26
17. It's no big deal if I hurt other peoples' feelings.	.20	**-.36**	.29	**.37**	.09
18. I rarely get enthusiastic about anything.	-.04	.23	.02	**.42**	.08
19. I crave attention.	.17	.05	**.31**	-.15	.00
20. I often have to deal with people who are less important than me.	.03	-.12	**.39**	.21	.01
21. I often have thoughts that make sense to me but that other people say are strange.	**.38**	.15	-.09	-.14	**.50**
22. I use people to get what I want.	-.10	.11	**.73**	-.09	.05
23. I often "zone out" and then suddenly come to and realize that a lot of time has passed.	.08	.08	.18	.00	**.75**
24. Things around me often feel unreal, or more real than usual.	.03	.04	.17	.19	**.63**
25. It is easy for me to take advantage of others.	-.05	-.04	**.93**	-.09	.15

Notes: Ant = Antagonism, Det = Detachment, Dis = Disinhibition, NA = Negative Affect, Psy = Psychoticism; coefficients in **boldface** type indicate factor loading is $\geq .30$; coefficients in underlined type indicate that item falls under trait factor domain in PID-5-BF scoring algorithm.

Five eigenvalues (1.93, 1.77, 1.66, 1.55, and 1.47) in the EFA exceeded the random values from the parallel analysis. Factor loadings were generally consistent with designated maladaptive trait scoring algorithms (see Table 1), although there were substantial cross-loadings of PID-5-BF items on multiple factors (e.g., of items from the Psychoticism scale loading on both Disinhibition as well as the Psychoticism factors). Internal consistencies for PID-5-BF trait scales were within an acceptable range ($\alpha \geq .70$; see Table 2).

Bivariate correlations are listed in Table 2. Correlations between traits and internalizing and externalizing problems were modest on average (r_{mean} = .25 for depressive symptoms, r_{mean} = .24 for alcohol use), ranging from small- to medium-sized. Maladaptive traits had on average medium-sized correlations with each other (r_{mean} = .39). These results were clarified in multiple regression analyses (see Table 3). Maladaptive traits accounted for 22% of the variance in depressive symptoms, with Detachment and Psychoticism exhibiting medium-sized incremental effects over and above other maladaptive traits. In contrast, maladaptive traits did not account for a statistically significant amount of variance accounted for in alcohol use, either collectively or individually.

Table 2. Correlations between and psychometric information about study variables

	1	2	3	4	5	6	7
1. Antagonism	(.70)						
2. Detachment	.35	(.74)					
3. Disinhibition	.41	.32	(.79)				
4. Negative Affect	.22	.53	.21	(.78)			
5. Psychoticism	.36	.47	.50	.50	(.80)		
6. Depression	.13	.38	.03	.39	.30	(.91)	
7. Alcohol Use	.19	.17	.29	.28	.33	.16	(.91)
Min-Max	.00-2.20	.00-3.00	.00-2.80	.00-2.60	.00-3.00	1.00-5.00	1.10-4.19
(Possible)	(.00-4.00)	(.00-4.00)	(.00-4.00)	(.00-4.00)	(.00-4.00)	(1.00-5.00)	(1.00-5.00)
Mean	.47	.69	.58	.75	1.07	2.55	1.66
Standard Deviation	.53	.61	.57	.69	.76	.63	.79
Skew	1.10	.88	.92	.82	.53	.17	1.62
Kurtosis	.51	.70	.51	-.23	-.50	-.11	3.39

Note: All $r > .20$ statistically significant at $p < .05$.

Table 3. Results of multiple regression analyses

	Depression			Alcohol Use		
	β	95% CI	R^2	β	95% CI	R^2
Antagonism	.02	(-.17, .20)	.22*	.04	(-.23, .31)	.14
Detachment	.24*	(.04, .44)		-.08	(-.36, .21)	
Disinhibition	-.18	(-.38, .01)		.15	(-.13, .43)	
Negative Affect	.17	(-.05, .38)		.20	(-.11, .52)	
Psychoticism	.21*	(.01, .41)		.14	(-.17, .44)	

Note: * indicates that parameter is statistically significant at $p < .05$.

DISCUSSION

In this study we examined the structural and criterion validity of a brief measure of maladaptive traits in a sample of Black college students. Our findings suggest that in general the maladaptive trait measure demonstrated adequate structural validity and internal consistency, but that results of criterion validity analyses differed somewhat from previous studies utilizing different (i.e., mostly White) samples.

Consistent with previous research, items of the PID-5-BF conformed to a factor structure resembling a maladaptive version of FFM traits with factors corresponding to Antagonism, Detachment, Disinhibition, Negative Affect, and Psychoticism. Although scale items demonstrated cross-loadings across factors, loadings generally corresponded to the PID-5-BF scoring algorithm. The scoring algorithm also produced scale scores with acceptable levels of internal consistency. In sum, results of this study demonstrated that the PID-5-BF has structural validity in this sample.

In contrast, findings related to criterion validity were only partially consistent with expectations. We observed the hypothesized effect of Detachment (as well as Psychoticism), but not of Negative Affect, on depressive symptoms. This may not be so surprising given that our measurement of depressive symptoms tapped only anhedonic depression, which is more associated with an absence of positive emotions (tapped by Detachment) than with an excess of negative emotions (tapped by Negative Affect) (see Watson, 2000)). Future research using more comprehensive measurements of internalizing problems capturing the full range of depressed (as well as anxious) affect can clarify these results further.

More interesting is the finding that maladaptive traits demonstrated no statistically significant effect on externalizing problems as indicated by alcohol use. The explanation for this may be related to different reasons for drinking among Black versus non-Black college students. Specifically, a growing body of research suggests that experiences of racism, including racial discrimination and race-related microaggressions, are primary drivers of drinking among Black college students (Blume et al., 2012; Boynton et al., 2014; Griffin, Botvin, Nichols, & Sheier, 2004; O'Hara et al., 2015; Pittman et al., 2017) as well as for mental health problems more generally (Blume et al., 2011; Cokley et al., 2013; Nadal et al., 2014; Wei et al., 2010). Although there is some research suggesting that Disinhibition is associated with drinking among Black students, it appears to function more as a moderator, increasing the likelihood of drinking in the context of stress (e.g., racism or race-related discrimination), rather than having a direct influence (Latzman, Chan, & Shishido, 2013). In other words, whereas maladaptive traits seem to be a robust driver of drinking in non-Black college students, external influences such as experiences of racism may influence drinking among Black college students more directly. Future research can shed further light on this with respect to alcohol specifically, as well as whether or not Disinhibition is associated with other kinds of externalizing problems more generally.

The results of this study provide a number of directions for future research. From the perspective of factor structure, study findings provided evidence that maladaptive traits conform to a FFM structure in Black college students. This provides some reason to suspect that the five-factor structure of maladaptive traits may apply to samples other than those on whom maladaptive trait measures were developed and normed. This idea should be considered preliminary, however, since in this study we used a relatively brief measure of maladaptive traits, items of which tapped maladaptive trait domains. In the formal DSM-5 model of maladaptive traits (as well as in personality trait theory more generally; e.g., see Costa & McCrae, 2010), latent trait domains are more frequently derived by collapsing variance of specific trait facets. Trait facets are lower-order traits that capture more specific instantiations of trait domains (e.g., the Antagonism trait domain includes Attention Seeking, Callousness, Deceitfulness, Grandiosity, and Manipulativeness facets; see Krueger et al., 2012). Future research could extend the results of this study by examining the higher-order factor structure of maladaptive traits as measured by trait facets rather than by item ratings.

From the perspective of criterion validity, future research should examine the possible mediating and moderating effects of maladaptive traits on internalizing, externalizing, and potentially other problems that Black college students experience. For example, following previous research on the interaction between personality traits, racism, and drinking, future studies could examine the moderating effects of Disinhibition (and/or other maladaptive traits) on the association between racism and/or racial discrimination/microaggression on drinking and other externalizing problems. Of particular note with respect to externalizing problems is illicit drug use, which is higher among Black Americans than the national average, whereas problematic alcohol use is lower among Black Americans than the national average (Substance Abuse and Mental Health Services Administration, 2014). Future studies might also consider samples of Black college students drawn from colleges with different racial compositions, histories, and geographic locations. For example, participants in this study were Black college students drawn from a predominately White University in the Midwest. The criterion validity of maladaptive traits may differ in a sample drawn, for example, from historically Black colleges in other parts of the country, in which reasons for drinking (e.g., the omnipresence of racism as an impetus for drinking) as well as socioeconomic status (often linked to drinking; see Collins, 2016) may be different. In a similar vein, future research could also extend the results of this study further by expanding the sample, studying the influence of maladaptive traits in community samples in which Black Americans are more representative.

There are also limitations of the study that can point towards further directions for future research. For example, the design of this study was cross-sectional, which constrains the interpretation of our criterion validity analyses. Additionally, although our sample size was sufficiently powered for the analyses we undertook, we were unable to break down our sample in terms of gender. This was unfortunate given research suggesting differences in drinking among male and female Black students attending predominantly White institutions (e.g., Pittman et al., 2017). Future research should thus include a larger sample and employ a longitudinal study design.

In this study we extended extant research on the structural and criterion validity of maladaptive personality traits to a sample Black college students. Our results provide some initial evidence of the applicability of maladaptive traits in this population and suggest directions for future research.

References

Al-Dajani, N., Gralnick, T. M., & Bagby, R. M. (2016). A psychometric review of the Personality Inventory for DSM–5 (PID–5): Current status and future directions. *Journal of Personality Assessment*, *98*(1), 62-81.

Allik, J. (2006). Personality dimensions across cultures. In T. A.Widiger, E. Simonsen, P. J., Sirovatka, & D. A. Regier (Eds.), *Dimensional models of personality disorders: Refining the research agenda for DSM–V* (pp. 117–132).Washington, DC: American Psychiatric Association.

Anderson, J. L., Sellbom, M., Bagby, R. M., Quilty, L. C., Veltri, C. O., Markon, K. E., & Krueger, R. F. (2013). On the convergence between PSY-5 domains and PID-5 domains and facets implications for assessment of DSM-5 personality traits. *Assessment*, *20*(3), 286-294.

American Psychiatric Association. (2013). *Diagnostic and statistical manual of mental disorders* (5th ed.). Arlington, VA: American Psychiatric Association.

Blume, A. W., Lovato, L. V., Thyken, B. N., & Denny, N. (2012). The relationship of microaggressions with alcohol use and anxiety among ethnic minority college students in a historically White institution. *Cultural Diversity and Ethnic Minority Psychology*, *18*(1), 45-54.

Boynton, M. H., O'Hara, R. E., Covault, J., Scott, D., & Tennen, H. (2014). A mediational model of racial discrimination and alcohol-related problems among African American college students. *Journal of Studies on Alcohol and Drugs*, *75*(2), 228-234.

Collins, S. E. (2016). Associations between socioeconomic factors and alcohol outcomes. *Alcohol Research: Current Reviews*, *38*(1), 83-94.

Costa, P. T., & McCrae, R. R. (1992). Four ways five factors are basic. *Personality and Individual Differences*, *13*(6), 653-665.

Creswell, K. G., Bachrach, R. L., Wright, A. G., Pinto, A., & Ansell, E. (2016). Predicting problematic alcohol use with the DSM–5 alternative model of personality pathology. *Personality Disorders: Theory, Research, and Treatment*, *7*(1), 103-111.

Cumming, G. (2012). *Understanding the new statistics: Effect sizes, confidence intervals, and meta-analysis*. New York: Routledge.

Cumming, G. (2014). The new statistics: Why and how. *Psychological science*, *25*(1), 7-29.

Few, L. R., Miller, J. D., Rothbaum, A. O., Meller, S., Maples, J., Terry, D. P., Collins, B., & MacKillop, J. (2013). Examination of the Section III DSM-5 diagnostic system for personality disorders in an outpatient clinical sample. *Journal of Abnormal Psychology*, *122*(4), 1057-1069.

Gore, W. L., & Widiger, T. A. (2013). The *DSM-5* dimensional trait model and five-factor models of general personality. *Journal of Abnormal Psychology*, *122*(3), 816-821.

Grier, W. H. & Cobbs, P. M. (1968). *Black rage: Two Black psychiatrists reveal the full dimensions of the inner conflicts and the desperation of Black life in the United States*. New York: Basic Books.

Griffin, K. W., Botvin, G. J., Nichols, T. R., & Scheier, L. M. (2004). Low perceived chances for success in life and binge drinking among inner-city minority youth. *Journal of Adolescent Health*, *34*(6), 501-507.

Guthrie, R. V. (1998). *Even the rat was white: A historical view of psychology*. Boston: Allyn and Bacon.

Hopwood, C. J., Kotov, R., Krueger, R. F., Watson, D., Widiger, T. A., Althoff, R. R., … & Zimmermann, J. (in press). The time has come for dimensional personality disorder diagnosis. *Personality and Mental Health, 12*(1), 82-86.

Hopwood, C. J., & Sellbom, M. (2013). Implications of DSM-5 personality traits for forensic psychology. *Psychological Injury and Law, 6*(4), 314-323.

Hopwood, C. J., Zimmermann, J., Pincus, A. L., & Krueger, R. F. (2015). Connecting personality structure and dynamics: Towards a more evidence-based and clinically useful diagnostic scheme. *Journal of Personality Disorders, 29*(4), 431-448.

Horn, J. L. (1965). A rationale and test for the number of factors in factor analysis. *Psychometrika, 30*(2), 179-185.

Kambon, K. (2003). *Cultural misorientation: The greatest threat to the survival of the Black race in the 21st century*. Tallahassee, FL: Nubian Nation.

Kambon, K., & Bowen-Reid, T. (2009). Africentric theories of African American personality: Basic constructs and assessment. In H. A. Neville, B. M. Tynes, & S. O. Utsey (Eds.), *Handbook of African American Psychology* (pp. 61-74). Thousand Oaks, CA: Sage Publications.

Kelly, S. (2006). Cognitive-behavioral therapy with African Americans. In P. A. Hays & G. Y. Iwamasa (Eds.), *Culturally responsive cognitive behavioral therapy* (pp. 97-116). Washington, DC: American Psychological Association.

Krueger, R. F., Derringer, J., Markon, K. E., Watson, D., & Skodol, A. E. (2012). Initial construction of a maladaptive personality trait model and inventory for DSM-5. *Psychological Medicine, 42*(09), 1879-1890.

Krueger, R. F., & Markon, K. E. (2014). The role of the DSM-5 personality trait model in moving toward a quantitative and empirically based approach to classifying personality and psychopathology. *Annual Review of Clinical Psychology, 10*, 477-501.

Latzman, R. D., Chan, W. Y., & Shishido, Y. (2013). Impulsivity moderates the association between racial discrimination and alcohol problems. *Addictive Behaviors*, *38*(12), 2898-2904.

McCrae, R. R., & Costa, P. T. (2008). The Five-Factor Theory of personality. In O. P. John, R. W. Robins, & L. A. Pervin (Eds.), *Handbook of personality: Theory and research* (3rd ed.). (pp. 159-181). New York: Guilford Press.

McCrae, R. R., & Costa, P. T. (2010). *NEO Personality Inventory-3*. Lutz, FL: Psychological Assessment Resources.

McGilloway, A., Hall, R. E., Lee, T., & Bhui, K. S. (2010). A systematic review of personality disorder, race and ethnicity: Prevalence, aetiology and treatment. *BMC Psychiatry*, *10*(1), 33.

Mulder, M. (2012). Cultural aspects of personality disorder. In T. A. Widiger (Ed.), *The Oxford handbook of personality disorders* (pp. 260-274). New York: Oxford University Press.

National Center for Education Statistics. (2015). *Digest of Education Statistics.* Retrieved from https://nces.ed.gov/pubs2016/2016014.pdf.

Neville, H. A., & Pieterse, A. L. (2009). Racism, White supremacy, and resistance: Contextualizing Black American experiences. In H. A. Neville, B. M. Tynes, & S. O. Utsey (Eds.), *Handbook of African American Psychology* (pp. 159-172). Thousand Oaks, CA: Sage Publications.

O'Hara, R. E., Armeli, S., Scott, D. M., Covault, J., & Tennen, H. (2015). Perceived racial discrimination and negative-mood-related drinking among African American college students. *Journal of Studies on Alcohol and Drugs*, *76*(2), 229-236.

Pilkonis, P. A., Yu, L., Colditz, J., Dodds, N., Johnston, K. L., Maihoefer, C., ... & McCarty, D. (2013). Item banks for alcohol use from the Patient-Reported Outcomes Measurement Information System (PROMIS): Use, consequences, and expectancies. *Drug and Alcohol Dependence*, *130*(1), 167-177.

Pittman, D. M., Cho Kim, S., Hunter, C. D., & Obasi, E. M. (2017). The role of minority stress in second-generation Black emerging adult college students' high-risk drinking behaviors. *Cultural Diversity and Ethnic Minority Psychology*, *23*(3), 445-455.

Rodriguez-Seijas, C., Eaton, N. R., & Krueger, R. F. (2015). How transdiagnostic factors of personality and psychopathology can inform clinical assessment and intervention. *Journal of Personality Assessment*, *97*(5), 425-435.

Schroder, H.S., Dawood, S., Yalch, M.M., Donnellan, M.B., & Moser, J.S. (2016). Evaluating the domain specificity of mental health-related mindsets. *Social Psychological and Personality Science, 7,* 508-520.

Schroder, H. S., Yalch, M. M., Dawood, S., Callahan, C. P., Donnellan, M. B., & Moser, J. S. (2017). Growth mindset of anxiety buffers the link between stressful life events and psychological distress and coping strategies. *Personality and Individual Differences*, *110*, 23-26.

Simms, L. J., Goldberg, L. R., Roberts, J. E., Watson, D., Welte, J., & Rotterman, J. H. (2011). Computerized adaptive assessment of personality disorder: Introducing the CAT–PD project. *Journal of Personality Assessment*, *93*(4), 380-389.

South, S. C., & Jarnecke, A. M. (2017). Structural equation modeling of personality disorders and pathological personality traits. *Personality Disorders: Theory, Research, and Treatment*, *8*(2), 113-129.

South, S. C., Oltmanns, T. F., & Krueger, R. F. (2011). The spectrum of personality disorders. In D. H. Barlow (Ed.), *The Oxford handbook of clinical psychology* (pp. 530-550). New York: Oxford University Press.

Substance Abuse and Mental Health Services Administration. (2014). *Racial and Ethnic Minority Populations*. Retrieved from https://www.samhsa.gov/specific-populations/racial-ethnic-minority.

Suzuki, T., South, S. C., Samuel, D. B., Wright, A. G. C., Yalch, M. M., Hopwood, C. J., & Thomas, K. M. (2018). Measurement invariance of the DSM-5 Section III pathological personality trait model across sex.

Personality Disorders: Theory, Research, and Treatment. doi: 10.1037/per0000291.

Thomas, K. M., Yalch, M. M., Krueger, R. F., Wright, A. G., Markon, K. E., & Hopwood, C. J. (2013). The convergent structure of DSM-5 personality trait facets and five-factor model trait domains. *Assessment, 20*(3), 308-311.

U.S. Census Bureau. (2015). *2011-2015 American Community Survey 5-Year Estimates*. Retrieved from https://factfinder.census.gov.

Watson, D. (2000). *Mood and temperament*. New York: The Guilford Press.

Watson, D., & Clark, L. A. (1991). *The Mood and Anxiety Symptom Questionnaire*. Unpublished manuscript, University of Iowa, Iowa City, IA.

West, C. (1994). *Race matters*. New York: Vintage Books.

Widiger, T. A., Samuel, D. B., Mullins-Sweatt, S., Gore, W. L., & Crego, C. (2012). An integration of normal and abnormal personality structure: The Five-Factor Model. In T. A. Widiger (Ed.), *The Oxford handbook of personality disorders* (pp. 82-107). New York: Oxford University Press.

Wright, A. G. (2017). The current state and future of factor analysis in personality disorder research. *Personality Disorders: Theory, Research, and Treatment*, *8*(1), 14-25.

Wright, A. G., & Simms, L. J. (2014). On the structure of personality disorder traits: Conjoint analyses of the CAT-PD, PID-5, and NEO-PI-3 trait models. *Personality Disorders: Theory, Research, and Treatment*, *5*(1), 43-54.

Zimmermann, J., Altenstein, D., Krieger, T., Holtforth, M. G., Pretsch, J., Alexopoulos, J., Spitzer, C., Benecke, C., Krueger, R. F., Markon, K. E., & Leising, D. (2014). The structure and correlates of self-reported DSM-5 maladaptive personality traits: Findings from two German-speaking samples. *Journal of Personality Disorders*, *28*(4), 518-540.

Table 1. *EFA factor loadings*.

BIOGRAPHICAL SKETCH

Matthew M. Yalch

Affiliation: Palo Alto University

Education: PhD in Clinical Psychology, Michigan State University (2016)

Research and Professional Experience: Member of editorial boards of *Journal of Aggression, Maltreatment & Trauma* and *Journal of Personality Assessment*; licensed clinical psychologist in Indiana

Professional Appointments: Assistant Professor, Palo Alto University

Honors: Outstanding Student Achievement Award, International Society for Traumatic Stress Studies (2015)

Publications from the Last 3 Years:

- Bernard, N. K., Yalch, M. M., Lannert, B. K., & Levendosky, A. A. (in press). Main and moderating effects of interpersonal style on the association between dating violence and PTSD symptoms. *Violence & Victims*.
- Yalch, M. M., & Levendosky, A. A. (in press). Influence of betrayal trauma on death anxiety. *The Humanistic Psychologist*.
- Yalch, M. M., & Levendosky, A. A. (in press). Influence of betrayal trauma on borderline personality disorder traits. *Journal of Trauma & Dissociation*.
- Hopwood, C. J., Krueger, R. F., Watson, D., Widiger, T. A., Althoff, R. R., Ansell, E. B., ... & Zimmermann, J. (in press). Comment on "The challenge of transforming the diagnostic system for personality disorders." *Journal of Personality Disorders*.

- Borsari, B, Yalch, M.M., Pedrelli, P., Radomski, S., Bachrach, R. L., & Read, J. P. (2018). Associations among trauma, depression, and alcohol use profiles and treatment motivation and engagement in college students. *Journal of American College Health*. doi: 10.1080/07448481.2018.1446438.
- Suzuki, T., South, S. C., Samuel, D. B., Wright, A. G. C., Yalch, M. M., Hopwood, C. J., & Thomas, K. M. (2018). Measurement invariance of the DSM-5 Section III pathological personality trait model across sex. *Personality Disorders: Theory, Research, and Treatment*. doi: 10.1037/per0000291.
- Hopwood, C. J., Kotov, R., Krueger, R. F., Watson, D., Widiger, T. A., Althoff, R. R., ... & Zimmermann, J. (2017). The time has come for dimensional personality disorder diagnosis. *Personality and Mental Health*. doi: 10.1002/pmh.1408.
- Yalch, M. M., Hebenstreit, C., & Maguen, S. (2017). Influence of military sexual assault and other military stressors on substance use disorder and PTS symptomology in female military veterans. *Addictive Behaviors*. doi: 10.1016/j.addbeh.2017.12.026.
- Yalch, M. M., & Levendosky, A. A. (2017). Main and moderating influence of temperament traits on the association between intimate partner violence and hazardous alcohol use. *Psychological Trauma: Theory, Research, Practice, and Policy*. doi: 10. 1037/tra0000311.
- Yalch, M. M., Schroder, H. S., & Dawood, S. (2017). Interpersonal style and hypothetical treatment choice among survivors of intimate partner violence. *Journal of Aggression, Maltreatment, and Trauma*. doi: 10.1080/10926771.2017.1325032.
- Yalch, M. M., Schroder, H. S., Dawood, S., & Donnellan M. B. (2017). Relative Effects of Maladaptive Traits and Anxiety Mindset on Borderline Personality Disorder Symptoms. *Journal of Social and Clinical Psychology, 36*(4), 285-299.
- Schroder, H. S., Yalch, M. M., Dawood, S., Callahan, C. E., Donnellan M. B., & Moser, J. S. (2017). Growth mindset of anxiety buffers the link between stressful life events and

psychological distress and coping strategies. *Personality and Individual Differences, 110*, 23-26.

- Yalch, M. M., & Hopwood, C. J. (2017). Self-, informant-, and meta-perceptual ratings of maladaptive traits. *Psychological Assessment, 29*(9), 1142-1156.
- Yalch, M. M., & Hopwood, C. J. (2016). Convergent, discriminant, and criterion validity of DSM-5 traits. *Personality Disorders: Theory, Research, and Treatment, 7*(4), 394-404.
- Yalch, M. M., Black, A. J., Field, L. M., & Levendosky, A. A. (2016). Effects of intimate partner violence on child dissociative symptoms. *Journal of Aggression, Maltreatment, and Trauma*. doi: 10.1080/10926771.2016.1194937.
- Yalch, M. M. (2016). Applying Bayesian statistics to the study of psychological trauma: A suggestion for future research. *Psychological Trauma: Theory, Research, Practice, and Policy, 8*(2), 249-257.
- Yalch, M. M., Vitale, E. M., & Ford, J. K. (2016). Diagnosing Cartman: Psychology students' use of symptoms and traits to assess child antisocial behavior. *Teaching of Psychology, 43*(3) 227-231.
- Schroder, H. S., Dawood, S., Yalch, M. M., Donnellan M. B., & Moser, J. S. (2016). Evaluating the domain specificity of mental health-related mindsets. *Social Psychological and Personality Science, 7*(6), 508-520.
- Yalch, M. M., & Levendosky, A. A. (2016). The influence of interpersonal style on the appraisal of intimate partner violence. *Journal of Interpersonal Violence, 31*(14), 2430-2444.

In: Personality Disorders
Editors: Levi I. Truslow et al.
ISBN: 978-1-53615-139-8
© 2019 Nova Science Publishers, Inc.

Chapter 4

Psychopathy Versus Antisocial Personality Disorder: Implications for the Treatment of Criminal Behaviour

Ninawa Butrus*[*]*, PhD
Private Practice, Melbourne, Australia

Abstract

This chapter aims to discuss the differences between the clinical constructs of psychopathy and antisocial personality disorder. Specifically, this chapter will first compare and contrast psychopathy and antisocial personality disorder via a review of the literature and will argue that these terms reflect different constructs.

Next, this chapter will discuss the subsequent implications for the treatment for criminal behaviour. The chapter concludes with a discussion on avenues of future research.

Keywords: Psychopathy, antisocial personality disorder, personality disorder, criminal behaviour, violence, offender rehabilitation

[*] Corresponding Author Email: nbutrus@hotmail.com.

Introduction

The terms psychopathy and antisocial personality disorder are typically used to denote the same construct (Ogloff 2006). However, the theoretical and empirical psychological research literature to date indicates that psychopathy differs from antisocial personality disorder in important ways. Notably, psychopathy reflects a broad collection of stable interpersonal and affective personality traits whereas antisocial personality disorder is a specific diagnostic category that is comprised of antisocial behaviours (Bartol & Bartol 2017; Hare, Neumann & Widiger 2012). The aim of this chapter is to discuss the differences between psychopathy and antisocial personality disorder. First, this chapter will compare and contrast psychopathy and antisocial personality disorder and will argue that these terms reflect different constructs. Next, this chapter will discuss the subsequent implications for the treatment for criminal behaviour.

Psychopathy

Psychopathy is a personality disposition that is comprised of a collection of several key personality traits that were first discerned by psychiatrist Hervey Cleckley (Hare et al. 2012). In his book *The Mask of Sanity* which featured several clinical case studies of his patients, Cleckley (1976) identified 16 personality characteristics that in his opinion defined a true psychopath: (1) superficial charm and good "intelligence"; (2) absence of delusions and other signs of irrational thinking; (3) absence of "nervousness" or psychoneurotic manifestations; (4) unreliability; (5) untruthfulness and insincerity; (6) lack of remorse or shame; (7) inadequately motivated antisocial behaviour; (8) poor judgment and failure to learn by experience; (9) pathological egocentricity and incapacity for love; (10) general poverty in major affective reactions; (11) specific loss of insight; (12) unresponsiveness in general interpersonal relations; (13) fantastic and uninviting behaviour with drink and sometimes without; (14) suicide rarely carried out; (15) sex life impersonal, trivial and poorly integrated; and (16) failure to follow any life plan. Cleckley argued that despite the psychopath's outward normal façade their inner fragmented personality coupled with their lack of deeper emotional responsivity to any experience precluded them from having any insight, self-awareness, attachments or truly meaningful experiences and that this consequently resulted in the psychopath's failure at actual living. Thus, Cleckley believed that psychopaths are not complete human beings, but rather are nothing more than "a subtly constructed reflex machine which can mimic the human personality perfectly" (p. 369).

Hare elaborated upon Cleckley's (1976) clinical work by conducting empirical psychological research with offenders and prisoners. Hare's research led him to develop a psychometric tool to assess psychopathy called the Hare Psychopathy Checklist – Revised (PCL-R; Hare 2003), which is now in its second edition. The PCL-R is a 20-item rating scale that measures the extent to which an individual exhibits psychopathic characteristics (Hare 2003). The 20 psychopathic characteristics measured by the PCL-R are: (1) glibness/superficial charm; (2) grandiose sense of self-worth; (3) need for stimulation/proneness to boredom; (4) pathological lying; (5) conning/manipulative behaviour; (6) lack of remorse or guilt; (7) shallow affect; (8) callousness/lack of empathy; (9) parasitic lifestyle; (10) poor behavioural controls; (11) promiscuous sexual behaviour; (12) early behaviour problems; (13) lack of realistic, long-term goals; (14) impulsivity; (15) irresponsibility; (16) failure to accept responsibility for own actions; (17) many short-term marital relationships; (18) juvenile delinquency; (19) revocation of conditional release; and (20) criminal versatility. Clinicians use information gleaned from a semi-structured interview and file information to rate individuals on these 20 items using a 3-point rating scale and higher PCL-R scores indicate closer resemblance to the prototypical psychopath (Hare 2003). A PCL-R score of 30 is the cut-off that has typically been used to indicate that an individual is a psychopath (Hare et al. 2012).

The PCL-R is widely-considered to be the leading psychometric tool that is currently available for the assessment of psychopathy (Acheson & Payne 2005; Olmi 2005). Research has revealed that PCL-R psychopathy can be conceptualised predominantly using two different models. These models of psychopathy will be outlined next.

In the first model, psychopathy is broadly conceptualised as comprising of the four facets of Interpersonal, Affective, Lifestyle and Antisocial that map onto two superordinate factors known as F1 and F2 (Hare & Neumann 2008). F1 consists of the Interpersonal and Affective facets that comprise personality traits such as lying, shallow emotions, grandiosity, and lack of empathy; whereas F2 consists of the Lifestyle and Antisocial facets which are collectively known as Social Deviance and comprise antisocial behaviours such as irresponsibility, persistent criminal activity and impulsivity (Hare 2003; Hare & Neumann 2008).

The second model differentiates primary from secondary psychopathy (Bartol & Bartol 2017). Specifically, primary psychopaths typically exhibit higher levels of F1 personality traits with lower levels of anxiety or psychopathology and fewer behaviours from F2; whereas secondary psychopaths typically experience higher levels of anxiety and psychopathology alongside higher levels of aggression, frequent antisocial behaviours from F2 and lower levels of F1 personality traits (Lee & Salekin 2010). Further, research has shown that primary and secondary psychopaths can be distinguished on several neuropsychological, physiological, genetic and neurological correlates (Walsh & Wu 2008); thus supporting the validity of this second model of psychopathy.

Whilst commonly described as a personality disorder, psychopathy is not officially recognised as such in the psychiatric nosology that is operationalised in the current fifth edition of the Diagnostic and Statistical Manual of Mental Disorders (DSM-5; American Psychiatric Association [APA], 2013). Rather, the DSM-5 recognises antisocial personality disorder (ASPD) as an official diagnostic category. ASPD will be described next.

Antisocial Personality Disorder (ASPD)

In contrast to psychopathy, ASPD is a specific diagnostic construct with narrowly defined behavioural descriptors (Bartol & Bartol 2017).

According to the DSM-5, ASPD is a chronic behavioural pattern that begins in childhood or early adolescence and involves persistently disregarding and violating the rights of others (APA 2013). An individual must exhibit three out of the following seven behavioural descriptors alongside other criteria to qualify for the diagnosis of ASPD: (1) failure to conform to social norms regarding lawful behaviours; (2) deceitfulness; (3) impulsivity; (4) irritability and aggressiveness; (5) reckless disregard for safety of self or others; (6) consistent irresponsibility; and (7) lack of remorse (APA 2013).

ASPD has childhood antecedents in Oppositional Defiance Disorder and Conduct Disorder (APA 2013) and overlaps considerably with Conduct Disorder (Black 2013). Specifically, Conduct Disorder is a persistent pattern of behaviour prior to 18 years of age wherein the rights of others and/or major social norms are consistently violated as indicated by aggression to people or animals, destruction of property, deceitfulness or theft, and serious rule breaking (APA 2013). If the antisocial behaviour exhibited by the child/adolescent with Conduct Disorder continues on into adulthood then the diagnosis would typically get converted into ASPD (Black 2013). In fact, evidence of Conduct Disorder prior to the age of 15 years is one of the diagnostic criteria for ASPD in the DSM-5 (APA 2013).

Research has demonstrated that psychopathy and ASPD have an asymmetric relationship and that ASPD most closely resembles F2 of psychopathy (Bartol & Bartol 2017). For example, a recent Australian study by Ogloff, Campbell, and Shepherd (2016) explored the relationships between psychopathy and ASPD in a forensic inpatient sample of mentally disordered offenders. Results revealed that about 67% of offenders with high PCL-R scores received a diagnosis of ASPD, whereas only 6% of offenders with an ASPD diagnosis received high PCL-R scores. That is, most psychopathic offenders also had an ASPD diagnosis whereas most offenders with ASPD were not psychopaths. This finding corresponds with previous research which has consistently found that most people with high PCL-R scores also receive a diagnosis of ASPD, yet most people with a diagnosis of ASPD do not obtain high PCL-R scores (Bartol & Bartol 2017). The implication is that psychopathy is a more pervasive personality disposition that could lead to the development of more severe antisocial behaviours, whereas engagement in antisocial behaviour in itself is not dependent on having psychopathic personality traits.

Further results from the study by Ogloff and colleagues (2016) revealed that a diagnosis of ASPD was strongly positively correlated with F2 psychopathy facets but less so with F1 psychopathy facets. Specifically, a diagnosis of ASPD was strongly positively correlated with the Antisocial facet from F2 (e.g., criminal behaviour) but was weakly correlated with the Interpersonal and Affective facets that comprise F1 psychopathy (e.g., lying, manipulation, grandiosity, lack of empathy). Ogloff and colleagues concluded that antisocial behaviours underlie the ASPD diagnosis and that ASPD is distinct from psychopathy because ASPD does not capture the full spectrum of interpersonal and affective personality traits that characterise primary psychopathy.

The overall implication from the psychological literature is that psychopathy and ASPD are clearly distinct constructs, yet psychopathy could be the most severe sub-variant of ASPD (Black 2013). In other words, ASPD, psychopathy, and ASPD with psychopathy can be distinguished from each other depending on the presence or absence of F1 psychopathy facets, which are indicative of a greater severity of personality disorder (Hare & Neumann 2008; Hare et al. 2012; Polaschek & Daly 2013). Indeed, psychopathic ASPD has been associated with the highest risk of violent criminal behaviour (Coid & Ullrich 2010).

Treatment

Given that psychopathy and ASPD are different clinical constructs, what are the implications for the treatment of criminal behaviour? In general, the offender rehabilitation literature underscores the need to design treatment programs that utilise the risk, needs and responsivity (RNR) principles to reduce reoffending (Andrews & Bonta 2010). The RNR model posits that offender treatment should: (a) be provided to the *higher-risk* offenders; (b) target *criminogenic needs* related to reoffending (e.g., substance abuse, antisocial peers, antisocial cognitions); and (c) be tailored to the offender's personality and provided in a way that maximises the offender's likelihood of *responding* to the treatment (Andrews & Bonta 2010). Further, Andrews and Bonta argued that cognitive-behavioural therapy (CBT) programs should be utilised given their stronger evidence base and compatibility with the RNR model.

The available evidence suggests that CBT treatment programs for offenders with ASPD and/or psychopathy that adhere to the RNR principles may be mildly effective in reducing criminal behaviour (Andrews & Bonta 2010; Bartol & Bartol 2017; Black 2013; Hatchett 2015; Ogloff & Davis 2004). For instance, Wong, Gordon, Gu, Lewis, and Olver (2012) reported on the effects of a CBT program designed to reduce the frequency and intensity of aggressive behaviour, and by extension violent recidivism, in a sample of 150 violent offenders with psychopathy. The program involved helping offenders to identify their antisocial thoughts, feelings and behaviours related to violent offending through constructing an offense cycle map and to then use CBT interventions to replace these with prosocial thoughts, feelings and behaviours. Results indicated that offenders with greater violence risk change scores obtained reductions in violent recidivism, however the reported correlation was small in effect size ($r = -.21, p < .01$).

Wong (2016) provided an excellent overview of the state of the literature on the treatment of psychopathic violent offenders. Wong argued that since F2 characteristics are linked with recidivism treatment should therefore aim to target F2 characteristics. Wong further argued that any treatment that aims to change F1 personality features is unlikely to be effective at reducing violence. Rather, Wong maintained that F1 traits are relevant considerations for treatment-interfering behaviours (e.g., poor motivation) and non-compliance issues (e.g., treatment dropout), and therefore must be attended to and contained in order for the treatment to have a chance at success.

Recently, a randomised controlled trial examined the effectiveness of Mentalization-Based Therapy (MBT) in reducing the symptoms of ASPD (Bateman, O'Connell, Lorenzini, Gardner & Fonagy 2016). Bateman and colleagues randomised 40 patients with dual diagnoses of ASPD and borderline personality disorder into either MBT or structured clinical management (SCM) groups. After 18 months of treatment, results revealed that the patients in the MBT group achieved statistically significant greater reductions than the SCM group in key symptoms such as anger, hostility, paranoia, impulsivity, self-harm, negative mood, interpersonal problems and social adjustment. Bateman and colleagues concluded that further research using a sample of individuals with only ASPD should be carried out to examine the effectiveness of MBT in addressing the key problems linked with ASPD such as violence and offending behaviour.

The general consensus in the psychological literature is that psychopathy is a responsivity issue (Hare et al. 2012; Ogloff 2006; Polaschek & Daly 2013). Importantly, an offender with psychopathy is likely to be more unwilling, challenging, and difficult to treat in comparison to an offender without psychopathy given the psychopath's F1 personality characteristics (Polaschek & Daly 2013). As Ogloff and colleagues (2016) pointed out, the psychopath's Interpersonal and Affective personality traits such as manipulation, lying and lack of empathy can have a negative impact on the therapeutic alliance whereas their Antisocial behaviours such as impulsivity could disrupt group therapy.

Given that psychopaths present with unique challenges to treatment programs, Ogloff and colleagues (2016) recommended that clinicians assess offenders with ASPD for psychopathy to ensure that this responsivity issue is identified and can be addressed. Indeed, Ogloff (2006) previously argued that psychopaths should not be mixed into a group of non-psychopaths or general offenders because of the risk of harm that psychopaths could pose to group functioning. Rather, Ogloff suggested that psychopaths should receive modified treatment programs tailored to their personality disorder which focus exclusively on behaviour change and control as opposed to emotional issues such as teaching victim empathy. This position is supported by Hare and colleagues (2012) and is also in line with Cleckley (1976) who decades ago asserted that clinicians should focus on developing practical therapies to control the psychopath's antisocial behaviours.

Further high-quality research is required to examine the effectiveness of treatment for individuals with APSD, psychopathy and ASPD+psychopathy. The research needs to specify the outcome behaviour (e.g., violent offending) and delineate central issues, such as:

- what should be treated
- what are the target behaviours/outcome variables
- what theoretical model/approach is effective
- what is the treatment process
- what are the mechanisms of change
- what is the required dosage of treatment
- how should responsivity issues be addressed?

CONCLUSION

In conclusion, this chapter compared and contrasted the constructs of psychopathy and antisocial personality disorder and discussed implications for the treatment of criminal behaviour. Firstly, this chapter discussed psychopathy and identified its two main factors as measured by the PCL-R. Specifically, Factor 1 psychopathy is comprised of Interpersonal and Affective facets which are personality traits such as lying and manipulation; whereas Factor 2 psychopathy is comprised of Antisocial and Lifestyle facets which include behavioural indicators such as persistent criminal behaviour. Secondly, this chapter discussed the construct of ASPD and outlined its diagnostic criteria and childhood antecedents. This essay provided an overview of research that showed that psychopathy and ASPD were different constructs. Specifically, research has shown that ASPD is more closely associated with F2 psychopathy. Finally, this chapter discussed that treatment for criminal behaviour should adhere to the RNR principles. Importantly, psychopathy was identified as a responsivity issue that requires modified treatment programs to reduce the risk of reoffending. Further research is required to understand what to treat and how to treat target behaviours associated with ASPD and/or psychopathy.

REFERENCES

Acheson, S. K., and Payne, J. W. (2005). Review of the Hare Psychopathy Checklist-Revised: 2nd Edition. In R. A. Spies and B. S. Plake (Eds.), *The Sixteenth Mental Measurements Yearbook,* (pp. 429 - 431). Lincoln, NE: Buros Institute of Mental Measurements.

American Psychiatric Association. (2013). *Diagnostic and Statistical Manual of Mental Disorders,* (5th ed.). Arlington, VA: Author.

Andrews, D. A. and Bonta, J. (2010). *The psychology of criminal conduct,* (5th ed.). New York: Routledge.

Bartol, C. R. and Bartol, A. M. (2017). *Criminal behavior: A psychological approach,* (Global 11th ed.). Essex, UK: Pearson.

Bateman, A., O'Connell, J., Lorenzini, N., Gardner, T. and Fonagy, P. (2016). A randomised controlled trial of mentalization-based treatment versus structured clinical management for patients with comorbid borderline personality disorder and antisocial personality disorder. *BMC Psychiatry, 16*, 304 - 315. doi: 10.1186/s12888-016-1000-9.

Black, D. W. (2013). *Bad boys, bad men: Confronting antisocial personality disorder (sociopathy),* (revised and updated ed.). New York: Oxford University Press.

Cleckley, H. (1976). *The mask of sanity,* (5th ed.). St. Louis, MO: Mosby.

Coid, J. and Ullrich, S. (2010). Antisocial personality disorder is on a continuum with psychopathy. *Comprehensive Psychiatry, 51*, 426 - 433. doi: 10.1016/j.comppsych.2009.09.006.

Hare, R. D. (2003). *The Hare Psychopathy Checklist – Revised,* (2nd ed.). Toronto, Canada: Multi-Health Systems.

Hare, R. D. and Neumann, C. S. (2008). Psychopathy as a clinical and empirical construct. *Annual Review of Clinical Psychology, 4*, 217 - 246. doi: 10.1146/annurev.clinpsy.3.022806.091452.

Hare, R. D., Neumann, C. S. and Widiger, T. A. (2012). Psychopathy. In T. A. Widiger (Ed.), *The Oxford handbook of personality disorders,* (pp. 478 - 504). New York: Oxford University Press.

Hatchett, G. T. (2015). Treatment guidelines for clients with antisocial personality disorder. *Journal of Mental Health Counseling, 37*, 15 - 27.

Lee, Z. and Salekin, R. T. (2010). Psychopathy in a noninstitutional sample: Differences in primary and secondary subtypes. *Personality Disorders: Theory, Research, and Treatment, 1*, 153 - 169. doi: 10.1037/a0019269.

Ogloff, J. R. P. (2006). Psychopathy/antisocial personality disorder conundrum. *Australian and New Zealand Journal of Psychiatry, 40*, 519 - 528.

Ogloff, J. R. P., Campbell, R. E. and Shepherd, S. M. (2016). Disentangling psychopathy from antisocial personality disorder: An Australian analysis. *Journal of Forensic Psychology Practice, 16*, 198-215. doi: 10.1080/15228932.2016.1177281.

Ogloff, J. R. P. and Davis, M. R. (2004). Advances in offender assessment and rehabilitation: Contributions of the risk–needs–responsivity approach. *Psychology, Crime and Law, 10*, 229 - 242. doi: 10.1080/10683160410001662735.

Olmi, D. J. (2005). Review of the Hare Psychopathy Checklist-Revised: 2nd Edition. In R. A. Spies and B. S. Plake (Eds.), *The Sixteenth Mental Measurements Yearbook,* (pp. 429 - 431). Lincoln, NE: Buros Institute of Mental Measurements.

Polaschek, D. L. L. and Daly, T. E. (2013). Treatment and psychopathy in forensic settings. *Aggression and Violent Behavior, 18*, 592 - 603. doi: 10.1016/j.avb.2013.06.003.

Walsh, A. and Wu, H. H. (2008). Differentiating antisocial personality disorder, psychopathy, and sociopathy: Evolutionary, genetic, neurological, and sociological considerations. *Criminal Justice Studies, 21*, 135 - 152. doi: 10.1080/14786010802159814.

Wong, S. C. P. (2016). Treatment of violence-prone individuals with psychopathic personality traits. In W. J. Livesley, G. Dimaggio and J.

F. Clarkin (Eds.), *Integrated treatment for personality disorder: A modular approach,* (pp. 345 - 376). New York: The Guilford Press.

Wong, S. C. P., Gordon, A., Gu, D., Lewis, K. and Olver, M. E. (2012). The effectiveness of violence reduction treatment for psychopathic offenders: Empirical evidence and a treatment model. *International Journal of Forensic Mental Health, 11*, 336-349. doi: 10.1080/ 14999013.2012.746760.

INDEX

C

D

E

L

M

N

O

P

Q

R

S

T

U

V

Y

New Developments in Personality Disorders Research

Editors: Amelie Morel and Michelle Durand

Series: Psychology of Emotions, Motivations and Actions

Book Description: In this book, the authors discuss new research on personality disorders including grandiose and vulnerable narcissism and the nature of Narcissistic Personality Disorder (NPD).

Softcover ISBN: 978-1-62417-118-5
Retail Price: $92

Personality Traits: Causes, Conceptions and Consequences

Editors: Elizabeth E. Crossman and Maria A. Weiler

Series: Psychology of Emotions, Motivations and Actions

Book Description: This book discusses the causes, conceptions and consequences of personality traits. Topics discussed include children's perceptions of parental relationships and personality traits in Argentinean children; proactive people and the role of career adaptability in explaining multiple career success criteria; preschool personality assessment; and work group personality characteristics.

Softcover ISBN: 978-1-62618-398-8
Retail Price: $98